INSTRUCTIONS TO USE:

1. The battery is not needed for operation of this.

2. Be holding the book with your hands, as it is show in the illustrations.

3. Make always sure, that you read the lines from reft to light, moving always from the top to bottom on the each page. Except that you may look at any pictures if you wish.

IMPORTANT

- USE ONLY AS DIRECTED
- DO NOT DRIVE OR OPERATE MACHINERY WHILE READING
- SHOULD DROWSINESS OCCUR, WE WOULDN'T BE A BIT SURPRISED
- DO NOT INDUCE VOMITING—THE CONTENTS WILL TAKE CARE OF THAT

The characters in this work are imaginary. Any resemblance to actual persons, living or dead, is purely coincidental. Void where taxed or prohibited by law. All sales are final. Not legal for trade. Do not remove this tag under penalty of law. Close cover before striking. Keep away from children. Actual mileage may vary. Close-captioned for the hearing impaired. Dispose of properly. An equal opportunity employer (M/F/H/Q/Z/R/S/L). All times Eastern Standard. Allow 4–6 weeks for delivery. Substantial penalty for early withdrawal. This bag is not a toy. Simulated TV reception. A paid political announcement. Alcohol 0% by volume. No purchase is necessary; you need not be present to win. Do not puncture, incinerate, or store above 451° F. Severe tire damage. Package not child-resistant. Author carries no cash. No step. For prevention of disease only. Post office will not deliver mail without postage. Objects in mirror are closer than they appear. This door must remain unlocked during business hours. Unleaded gasoline only. Member FDIC.

> ## WARNING: The Attorney General Has Determined That Books May Contain Harmful or Dangerous Ideas

This product is sold by weight, not by volume. Jokes may have settled slightly during shipping.

Best when read before AUG '91

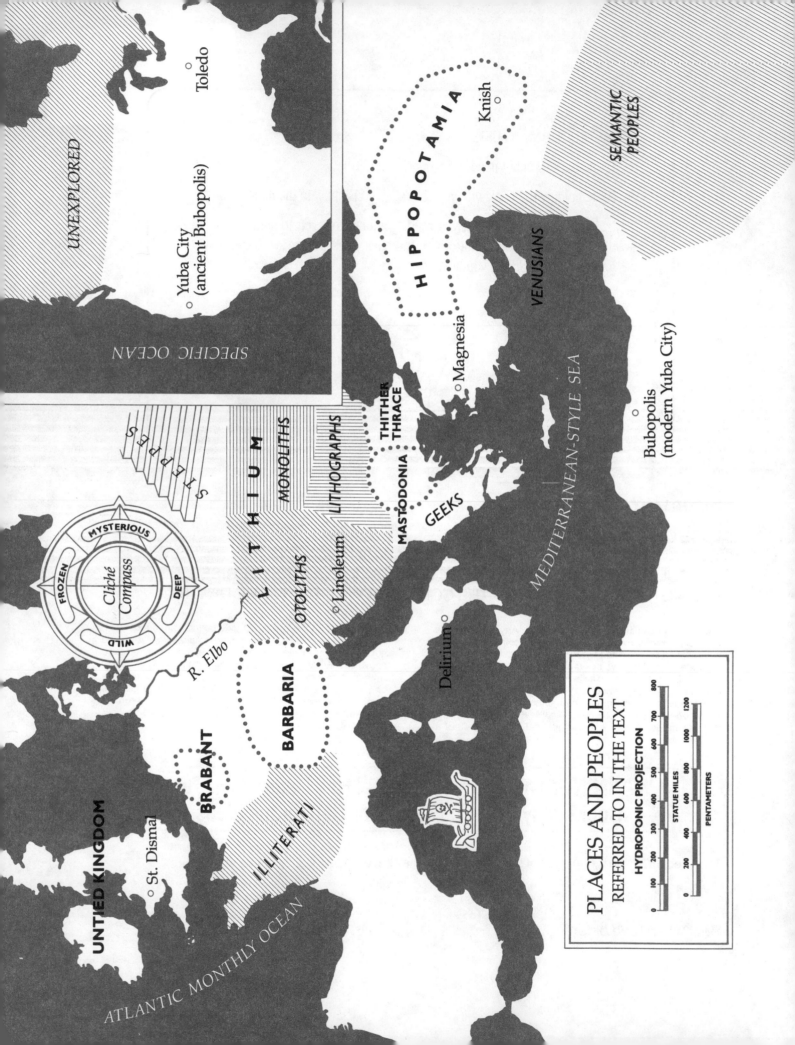

CVLTVRE
MADE·STVPID

Written and Illustrated by Tom Weller

IN STEREO
Where Available

Houghton Mifflin Company · Boston · 1987

EDITOR'S NOTE: This work contains material from classic works of art and literature of past eras. In many cases, social attitudes towards vegetables have changed over the centuries; terms and concepts which today would be considered offensive were once commonplace. In light of the historic importance of these works, where such questionable references to vegetables occur they are reproduced unexpurgated.

The sole exceptions are certain words referring to legumes which are no longer acceptable and appear here replaced by dashes.

Library of Congress Cataloging-in-Publication Data

Weller, Tom.
Culture made stupid.

1. Civilization — Anecdotes, facetiae,
satire, etc.   I. Title.
PN6231.C46W45   1987   818'5402   87-3982
ISBN 0-395-40461-4 (pbk.)

Printed in the United States of America

BTA 10 9 8 7 6 5 4 3 2 1

Contents

Introduction

W HAT IS "CVLTVRE"? Not the same as "culture," which a dish full of germs has. Not the same as the anthropologist's "culture," which even people with bones in their noses have. No, cvltvre is something nobler, loftier, finer, thicker with pompous adjectives.

To know cvltvre is to know the market value of a painting, the name of a piece of music, an amusing anecdote about history, what the reviewers said about a book or film.

Many people hesitate to take up art, literature, or philosophy because they believe it requires "intelligence." Others fear that years of arduous study will be required.

Nothing could be further from the truth! In fact, you need only know a handful of buzzwords, stock phrases, and conventional concepts. Thousands have produced public TV documentaries, become newspaper film critics, received lucrative government grants, written best-selling books, and lost up to fifty pounds of unwanted fat—with no more knowledge of their subjects than is contained in these pages.

With its handy tables and short summaries, this book can provide you with a complete cvltvral background—a background equal to that of many graduates of prestigious universities—in only minutes!

CATASTROPHE
muse of
awards
telecasts

ANESTHESIA
muse of
crossword
puzzles

EUCHRE
muse of
card tricks

DICHONDRA
muse of
pruning

Here's a little test to see if you, yes *you*, are a candidate for cvltvre. Let's imagine two couples: Jason and Jennifer, who live in a nice house in an affluent suburb; and Merle and Maxine, who reside at a trailer park in Yuba City, CA. What would we see if we looked inside their homes?

	MERLE & MAXINE	JASON & JENNIFER
on the coffee table:	*Rod & Gun*	*Atlantic Monthly*
	Sears catalogue	Sharper Image catalogue
	religious tract	Wittgenstein's *Tractatus Logico-Philosophicus*
on the wall:	velvet painting of clown	Goines poster
on the mantel:	"Praying Hands" statuette	Pre-Columbian sculpture
on the TV:	"Celebrity Wrestling"	nothing; but the dial has been set to PBS, then removed
on the stereo:	*100 Polka Favorites*	*Talking Heads Play Hindemith's Greatest Hits*
in the kitchen:	Vegematic	Cuisinart
	electric can opener	electric pasta machine
in the fridge:	TV Dinners	squid
	Hostess Sno Balls	goat cheese
	Kool-Aid	Perrier
in the closet:	bowling shirts	running shoes
	plaid double knit suit	down jacket
in the bathroom:	musical toilet paper dispenser	cordless phone
in the back yard:	plastic wading pool	hot tub
	decorative border of hubcaps	redwood deck
in the front yard:	plastic flamingos	plastic flamingos

Which couple appeals to you more? If you said, "Yuba City, here I come," you can close this book right now, provided you've already paid for it. But if you said, "Yes, I'll have some of the grilled squid," then you're a potential consumer of cvltvre.

ANGOSTURA
muse of
blender drinks

ANATHEMA
muse of
novelizations

MIASMA
muse of
tax
accounting

PARAPHERNALIA
muse of
collectibles

TOYOTA
muse of
personalized
license plates

I. The Life of the Mind

I am that I am.
  —JEHOVAH
I yam what I yam.
  —POPEYE
I think, therefore I am.
  —DESCARTES
I think I can, I think I can.
  —THE LITTLE ENGINE THAT COULD

Socrates   *Plato*   *Aristotle*

THE HISTORY OF WESTERN THOUGHT does not, of course, start with the Greeks. But all books do.

The Greek philosophers began by asking fundamental questions about the nature of life, the universe, and thought itself. They soon discovered that the answers to these questions were not forthcoming, nor likely to be.

But in time, they made a greater discovery: that merely posing the questions—in a suitably convoluted manner—sounded mighty impressive. And a philosopher who sounded thus impressive got veneration, large fees, and comfortable consulting positions.

The **Pre-Socratics** were the first important school of thinkers. Their works survive in only a few brief fragments:

Nature abhors a vacuum cleaner.
   —Clitoris
You can't step in the same cow pie twice.
   —Asparagus
Many are called, but few are at home.
   —Zero

Among the survivals is Peristalsis's famous formulation of his dualistic theory of nature:

1. **What is, is.**
2. **What is not, is not.**
3. **Everything else is negotiable.**

After the Pre-Socratic thinkers came the Post-Socratics. (There were no actual "Socratics" except for Socrates—who may or may not have actually existed, as he himself would doubtless be the first to admit if he were alive today.)

The leading Post-Socratic was Plato, who wrote philosophical discourses in a form called the **dialogue**, even though one guy does all the talking. The following example is from the *Eurethra*.

Socrates: Surely, it is the case, is it not, that the many and the one cannot be the same?
Glaucoma: Yes, that is true, Socrates.
Socrates: And then is it not true also that the one and the many are likewise not the same?
Glaucoma: Undoubtedly so, Socrates.
Socrates: Then tell me, must not the one be considered identical with itself?
Glaucoma: Indeed, Socrates, no one could possibly deny it.
Socrates: And similarly the many with the many?

Glaucoma: Certainly, Socrates, you must be correct.
Socrates: And that which is not the same, must it not therefore be different?
Glaucoma: Surely, Socrates, that is the case.
Socrates: Therefore, Glaucoma, I propose to demonstrate, in the course of several more days of this dialogue, that the one and the many are different.
Glaucoma: Anybody here got any hemlock?

Here we must make note of the one surviving fragment by Plato's psychiatrist, who said, "The unanalyzed life is not worth living."

After Plato came Aristotle, who invented the **sillygism**, a powerful tool for logic. Here is an example:

All men are mortal.
All accounts of logic use the same stupid examples.
Therefore, at least you won't have to listen to them forever.

Aristotle also wrote extensively on politics, where he was able to apply his sillygistic technique to statecraft:

Society should be ruled by the best class.
I am middle class.
Therefore, society should be ruled by the middle class.

In addition, Aristotle is considered the father of modern science. He was the first to base his description of the world not on theory, but on what he actually observed around him. Today, this idea seems obvious; it strikes us as strange that nobody had ever thought of it before. And even stranger that nobody has ever thought of it since.

The Role of Rhetoric

The ancient world had a high regard for rhetoric. Together with grammar and logic, it formed the standard curriculum, called the **trivium.** Our word "trivial" is derived from trivium, and is still often applied to the content of higher education.

The trivium was the primary education of the public man. Today, of course, we wouldn't consider grammar, logic, and rhetoric an appropriate course of study for a political figure—grammar and logic having fallen out of fashion.

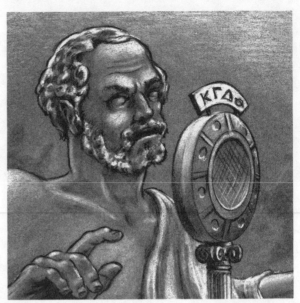

Demosthenes

COMMON RHETORICAL FIGURES

Prosthesis: to use words that are very hard to spell

Antithesis: to make fun of an opponent's doctoral dissertation

Argumentum ad mulierem: to buttress one's argument by asking one's wife for support

Tracheotomy: to prove an argument by saying, "Because I say so, that's why"

Amnesia: to repeat a word or phrase because you can't remember what you were going to say

Epilepsis: to draw out a word or phrase because you've dropped your notes on the floor

Hysteria: to begin a speech by telling a little joke you got from the utility company newsletter

Catachrome: to show a slide that has been put in the carousel upside down

Erotolepsis: to illustrate a point with an off-color anecdote

Diaspora: to deliver an introduction longer than the speech of the person introduced

Anastrophe: to ask a question of someone unable to answer, as, "If you can't hear me in the back there, raise your hands"

Antipasto: to abbreviate one's argument in anticipation of an approaching lunch break

The secondary set of ancient studies was called the **quadrivium** and consisted of arithmetic, geometry, astronomy, and I forget the other one — I think it was home ec. The trivium and quadrivium together were known as the seven liberal arts. Due to the threat of funding cuts under recent administrations, they are now usually called the seven non-partisan arts.

The high regard the Romans held for oratory is shown by Cicero's famous definition of an orator: *vir bonus, dicendi peritus* — "a good man, if I do say so myself."

Demosthenes was the greatest of all orators. Legend has it that he stammered badly as a youth. Determined to overcome his handicap, he began a stern regimen. Every day, he would go down to the sea-shore, fill his mouth with pebbles, and address the roaring surf.

When at last he could clearly enunciate over the ocean's roar, he switched to a tougher exercise. He would address crowds at the chariot races while his mouth was filled with golf balls.

Finally, he moved on to the ultimate challenge: speaking to a fourth grade recess while eating a peanut butter sandwich.

The skills he developed in this way came to fruition when he delivered his famous orations against Philip of Mastodon. His impassioned finale was a great crowd pleaser, as he declaimed the closing passages while drinking a glass of water.

THE FIRST LAWS: THE CODE OF HAMMURABI

It was a major step forward for Western civilization when men began to assemble written collections of laws. Such a body of laws is called a **code** because it is generally undecipherable. The earliest surviving example of a law code was promulgated by Hammurabi, who ruled Hippopotamia from 1728–1686 BC (Eastern Standard Time).

XV. If a man striketh another man [so as] to knock off his nose, his own nose shall be stricken off.

XVI. If a man striketh another man's slave [so as] to knock off his nose, he shall pay the slave's owner 100 silver *gonzagas*.

XVII. If a man striketh another man's wife [so as] to knock off her nose, he shall buy the man [a] beer and apologize sincerely.
[. . . .]

LIV. If a tree groweth on a neighbor's land, and if a branch of that tree extendeth over a man's property, and, because of rottenness, the branch falleth and striketh the man on the head, he shall be damned sorry.
[. . . .]

LIX. If a man's dog fouleth another man's lawn, the aggrieved man may gather the foul matter in a paper bag, place the paper bag on the other man's doorstep, set fire to [it], ring the doorbell, and run away.
[. . . .]

CIX. No shoes, no shirt, no suffrage.
[. . . .]

CLII. If a man eateth crackers in bed, and his wife no longer wisheth to continue with him, she may say "I divorce thee" three times, and bash his brains out with an ax, and she shall be considered free of him.

CLIII. If a child seeketh to become a musician and practiceth loudly in the house, or if a child groweth his hair in strange ways, his father may with impunity sell [him] into slavery.
[. . . .]

CCCLIV. No running by the pool.
[. . . .]

CCCLX. If a man seeketh to park his oxcart, and another man quickly occupieth the place before he can do so, the aggrieved man may let the air out of the other man's ox.
[. . . .]

CDXIX. Do not slouch, for it is [an] abomination; rather stand up straight. There, that's better. And comb your hair, it looks like a rat's nest.

CDXX. You really should floss more.

The Protestant Reformation

The Protestant Reformation began when Martin Luther nailed his Ninety-five Theses to the church door. The Church was outraged, feeling he could have used the bulletin board like everybody else. Also they felt that ninety-five theses were excessive, since God had only needed ten.

The Reformation and Counter-Reformation put an end to corrupt practices such as **simony**, or the selling of indulgences. The elimination of simony was a unique achievement for religion. Of course, the Church was the sole *cause* of this particular mortal sin. Still, it remains the only sin ever actually eradicated by Christianity.

The Renaissance

This great period saw the rise of the **Renaissance man**, a figure equally accomplished in all the arts and sciences. Renaissance man finally died out due to his lack of interest in Renaissance woman.

A crucial test of intellectual discourse is knowing when to use "Renaissance" and when to use "renascence." Unfortunately, the subject is too complicated to cover here. A good rule of thumb is to use whichever one you think you might be able to spell.

Modern Thinkers

The important point to remember about philosophers of the modern period is that Berkeley is pronounced "Barkeley" (unless referring to the city, which is pronounced "Moscow").

On the whole, recent philosophers have been a more fun-loving lot than their predecessors. Friedrich Nietzsche created a popular cartoon character, "Superman"; Marx once found Georg Wilhelm Friedrich Hegel standing on his head; and Karl Marx himself, of course, was a vaudeville comedian, although he retired from the stage earlier than his famous brothers.

One of the more remarkable modern

THE BIBLE AT A GLANCE

When: 4004 BC–AD 96

Where: North Africa, the Near East, the Mediterranean

Major Characters: Adam, Eve, Cain, Abel, Noah, Shem, Ham, Japheth, Abraham, Lot, Sarah, Isaac, Ishmael, Rebekah, Esau, Jacob, Rachel, Laban, Joseph, Judah, Benjamin, Moses, Aaron, Balaam, Joshua, Caleb, Deborah, Gideon, Samson, Delilah, Ruth, Naomi, Boaz, Samuel, Eli, Saul, David, Goliath, Absalom, Solomon, Bathsheba, Hiram, Elijah, Jezebel, Elisha, Isaiah, Cyrus, Ezra, Darius, Nehemiah, Ahasuerus, Esther, Job, Jeremiah, Ezekiel, Daniel, Nebuchadnezzar, Mary, Joseph, Jesus, John the Baptist, Salome, Herod, Mary Magdalene, Lazarus, Peter, Pontius Pilate, Matthew, Mark, Luke, John, Paul, George, & Ringo

Phrases to Remember: Let there be light, Am I my brother's keeper?, Thou shalt not kill, Thy belly is like an heap of wheat set about with lilies, Do unto others as you would have others do unto you

Outline: Creation of the world, travails of the Jews, arrival of the Messiah

Theme: Self-improvement

thinkers is Claude Lévi-Strauss. Beginning his long career in San Francisco during the Gold Rush days, he developed the sturdy denim trousers that bear his name today. In the mid-twentieth century, he attempted to apply the same successful techniques to the study of anthropology. The result was "structuralism," a method that uses copper rivets to hold theories together. A major work is *The Pegged and the Flared*, in which he demonstrates his famous "shrink-to-fit" style of reducing data to suit an analytical scheme.

THE ROLE OF WOMEN

The masculine bias that pervades Western intellectual history has obscured the many important contributions by women. Here are some historical females who have been unduly neglected.

MATILDA THE HUN
The scourge of Europe in the fifth century. Her warriors were renowned for their ability with the bow —tying up their hair and gift-wrapping with equal dexterity.

SANDRA CLAUS
Mythological medieval saint who was thought to keep track of children's behavior all year long. She brought lumps of coal for bad little girls and pipe bombs for bad little boys.

RENÉE DESCARTES
Mathematician and philosopher; author of famous statement, "I think, therefore I am, I think." Developed Cartesian coordinates—a mix 'n' match wardrobe of skirts, blouses, and philosophies.

PAULA REVERE
Revolutionary War heroine who spread the word of an impending British attack by calling all her friends on the telephone.

SITTING COW
Chieftain of the Sue Indians. She defeated Georgia Custer in the battle of the Darling Little Big Horn.

ANNA PURNA
Intrepid explorer who conquered most of the world's tallest mountain climbers. She was the first to employ as guides the Sherpas' wives, the Herpas.

The American Experiment

The bicentennial of the U.S. Constitution reminds us of the stirring events surrounding the world's greatest experiment in self-government—the American republic.

A turning point in human history occurred when the oppressed American colonists dumped their tea into Boston harbor and switched to drinking coffee. The extra caffeine in coffee undoubtedly helped promote the active spirit vital to a free enterprise system. Tea is a thin, weak beverage and its use invariably leads to totalitarian socialism; witness the listless, oppressed state of the people in countries where it is used, such as the Soviet Union, China, and Britain.

Having overthrown colonial rule, the Founders were faced with devising a system of governance for the infant republic. (The Founders were formerly called the Founding Fathers, but the term has been changed to avoid sexism. The Founders remain entirely male, however.)

During its first years, the United States was governed by the Articles of Confed-

The Liberty Plug

eration. The articles were cut out of magazines and pasted in a scrapbook by Benjamin Franklin. Although he did a tidy job, it was felt that the new nation should have something more impressive.

The Constitution as we know it was framed by the Constitutional Convention in 1787 and hung on the wall the following year. Influential in its adoption was *The Federalist Papers*, in which the work of the Convention was lauded by three of its members writing under an assumed name.

The historic principles embodied in that original document are still revered today:
- Freedom of speech was guaranteed, except in the case of pornography, libel, or subversive material.
- The right to vote was extended to all, except women, slaves, children, and poor people.
- The people's right to bear arms was protected, unless it meant something else.
- Income taxes were prohibited.

Even the greatest document, however, must change with the times. Currently a call for a new constitutional convention

The Washington Monument

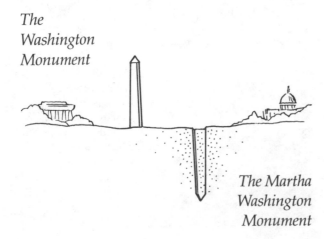

The Martha Washington Monument

16

is before many state legislatures. Many changes would be discussed at such a convention, chief among which is a proposed revision of the First Amendment. This amendment currently reads:

I. Congress shall make no law respecting an establishment of religion, or prohibiting the free exercise thereof; or abridging the freedom of speech or of the press; or the right of the people peaceably to assemble, and to petition the government for a redress of grievances.

Under the proposal, this amendment would simply be shortened:

I. Congress shall make no law.

This revision, while obviously preserving all the provisions of the original, would end most of the problems that have beset the nation in recent years, and save a lot of money as well.

SHOUTING "FIRE" IN A CROWDED THEATER: EXPERIMENTAL EVIDENCE

An important principle in First Amendment law was articulated by Oliver Wendell Holmes in a landmark decision (Schenck vs. United States, 249 U.S. 47 [1919]).[1] "The most stringent protection of free speech would not protect a man in falsely shouting fire in a theatre and causing a panic," wrote Justice Holmes. Though this example has formed the basis for many key rulings, it had never been tested in practice. Recently, however, a distinguished scholar undertook to examine the results of such an act in a rigorous scientific context.

Dr. Athol Swycaffer of the Department of Stress Management, Fourlane University, reported his intriguing results in the *Journal of Sociological Claptrap*. "What actually happens," Dr. Swycaffer asked, "when you shout 'fire' in a crowded theater?"

A sample of forty-seven movie theaters across the country was selected for the experiment. The sample was divided into a "test" group and three "control" groups. In the test group, a graduate student in the audience shouted "fire" at a randomly chosen point in the performance, and the results were observed and tabulated. In control group 1, patrons viewed the film under normal circumstances. In control group 2, an assistant shouted "fire," and then the theater was actually set ablaze. In control group 3, the theater was torched without any warning cry. Observers assigned the resultant behavior of the crowd a value on the Wassenberg-Schevitsky Panic Scale.

The results proved highly susceptible to influence from particular test conditions. For instance, subjects watching Sylvester Stallone or Chuck Norris films proved relatively impervious to the shouted warning. The experimenters noted that members of these audiences were already shouting "Fire!" as well as "Shoot!" and "Kill the commie creeps!" effectively drowning out the experimenter's shout.

Subjects in the "actual fire" groups showed expectedly higher scores in all categories. Interestingly, these theaters also showed 14% greater revenues from soft drink and popcorn sales.

A surprising result was the unexpectedly high scores for control group 1, the "normal" group. One injury occurred when a man was attacked and beaten by fellow patrons for continuously explaining the movie to his girlfriend in a loud voice. Three fatalities were caused by suffocation in the smaller multiplex cinemas, and a fourth by accidental inhalation of a Milk Dud. The remaining anomalous scores are due to two audiences that exhibited high panic levels when a sneak preview of a Barbra Streisand film was announced.

Encouraged by his results, Dr. Swycaffer is currently doing research in bars across the country in hopes of shedding light on the old proposition, "Your right to swing your fist stops where my nose begins," and is simultaneously recruiting adolescent subjects to test whether "If everyone else jumped off a cliff, would you do it too?"

---

1. This incomprehensible form of citation is used by lawyers to prevent clients from going to libraries and looking up the law for themselves.

GROUP	CONDITION	SAMPLE	PANIC RATING	INJURIES	FATALITIES
Test	warning, no fire	14	4.9	18	6
Control 1	no warning, no fire	13	4.5	11	5
Control 2	warning, fire	9	7.8	26	8
Control 3	no warning, fire	11	9.1	19	10
		47	6.6 (av.)	74	29

How to Talk Intellectual

If you want to *be* an intellectual, you have to *talk* like an intellectual. It all boils down to words and phrases. You've probably talked to people who used words you didn't know, or threw in quotations you'd never heard. Don't let them buffalo you!

Just remember this handy rule: ninety percent of the time, a word you've never heard before refers either to **a kind of African antelope** or **a disease of sheep**. For the remaining words, the speaker doesn't know what they mean either. It's that simple.

Likewise, remember that almost all quotations are either from Shakespeare or the Bible. The small fraction that aren't are from Bob Dylan songs.

When it's your turn to talk, you can't lose if you use the **three-part rule**; stay **au courant**, use the **power words**, and avoid the **stupid words.**

What do we mean by staying **au courant** (French for "with raisins")? This little chart should make it clear.

STAYING AU COURANT

The commonest error in speech is using old-fashioned words that have been replaced with improved equivalents.

OLD TERM	NEW TERM
sneakers	running shoes
underdeveloped country	less developed country
workmen's compensation	workers' compensation
Peking	Beijing
TV	monitor
instruction manual	documentation
retarded	special
macaroni	pasta

A trickier problem is staying on top of old terms that acquire new meanings.

TERM	OLD MEANING	NEW MEANING
ERA	earned run average	Equal Rights Amendment
CD	civil defense	compact disc or certificate of deposit
The Police	law enforcement agency	band
Matt Dillon	marshal of Dodge City	film actor
stereo	record player	TV
IRA	Irish Republican Army	Individual Retirement Account
Crockett & Tubbs	Davy & Wash	Sonny & Rico
two bits	quarter dollar	quarter byte

What about the **power words?** Well, there are certain words so powerful that everyone who hears them is impressed—*even when they're completely meaningless!* Pepper your speech with them, at random.

Finally, avoid the **stupid words**. There are some words in the English language so inherently silly that no one can ever take them seriously. Don't let these words creep into your speech or writing.

THE TEN POWER WORDS

heuristic	scenario
demographics	architectonic
gestalt	parameters
systems	stochastic
teleological	digital

THE TEN STUPIDEST WORDS IN THE ENGLISH LANGUAGE

nosegay	grout
garbanzo	blubber
grommet	snide
halibut	phlegm
fracas	cumquat

Using Graphs and Statistics

Graphs and statistics are an important part of intellectual discourse. Statistics, however fraudulent or irrelevant, lend an air of authority to any argument. When embodied in a graph or chart, they become even less comprehensible, and therefore more convincing. No wonder the average year's output of statistics, in the U.S. alone, would stretch four times around the earth at the equator.[1]

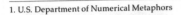

1. U.S. Department of Numerical Metaphors

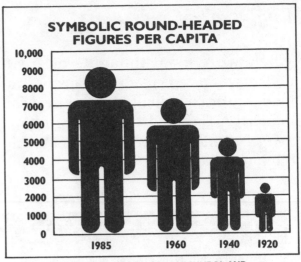

SOURCE: U.S. ASSOCIATION OF SYMBOL AND STICK FIGURE PRODUCERS

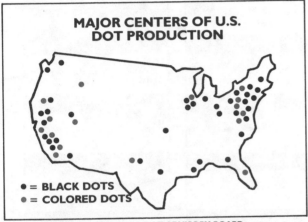

SOURCE: NATIONAL DOT ADVISORY BOARD

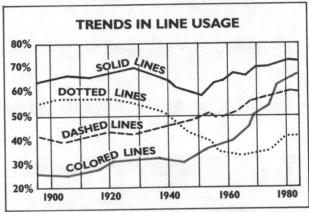

SOURCE: BUREAU OF STATISTICAL STATISTICS

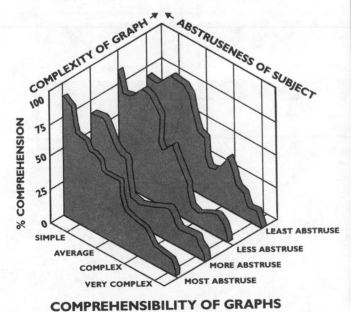

COMPREHENSIBILITY OF GRAPHS

SOURCE: AMERICAN GRAPH COUNCIL

EXAMPLES OF EFFECTIVE USE OF STATISTICS

• 50% of the U.S. population has a sub-median standard of living.

• The typical man or woman in the U.S. has 1 chance in 10 of becoming pregnant in the next year.

• The average mortality rate among people who jog is 100%.

• People who buy paperback humor books are much less likely to be eaten by crocodiles than the world population in general.

Dial-A-Thot

Below are great thoughts of great thinkers. You can create your own great thoughts by combining theirs. Just twist the Dial-A-Thot and drop the resulting *bon mot* into any conversation. People will think you're deep!

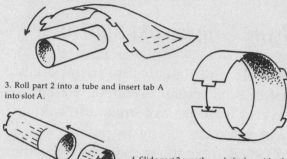

1. Cut out parts 1, 2, and 3 along the heavy black lines.
2. Glue part 1 around the core from a roll of bathroom tissue. Be sure that tabs B extend beyond the end of the tube.

3. Roll part 2 into a tube and insert tab A into slot A.

4. Slide part 2 over the end of tube, with tabs positioned as shown.

PART 1 / PART 2

PART 1	PART 2
Let me not to the marriage of true minds admit	impediments
Only the brave deserve the	fair
Those who cannot remember the past are condemned to	repeat it
Man is the measure of	all things
Art is long, life is	short
Here I stand; I can	do no other
The meek shall inherit the	earth
The die is	cast
If this be treason,	make the most of it
Patriotism is the last refuge of	scoundrels
Candy is dandy but liquor is	quicker
Things fall apart; the center cannot	hold
These are the times that try men's	souls
Less is	more
Music has charms to	soothe a savage breast
Give me liberty or give me	death
God is	dead
If music be the food of love,	play on
The unexamined life is not worth	living
That government is best which governs	least
If you seek a monument,	look around you
Beauty is truth, truth	beauty
To thine own self be	true
Buy low,	sell high

PARTS 3

DIAL A THOT

DIAL A THOT

5. Attach parts 3 to each end of tube by inserting tabs B into slots B on parts 3.

6. To generate great thoughts, twist ends in opposite directions until stripes align.

II. The Magic of Music

If music be the food of love, play "Melancholy Baby."
    —SHAKESPEARE

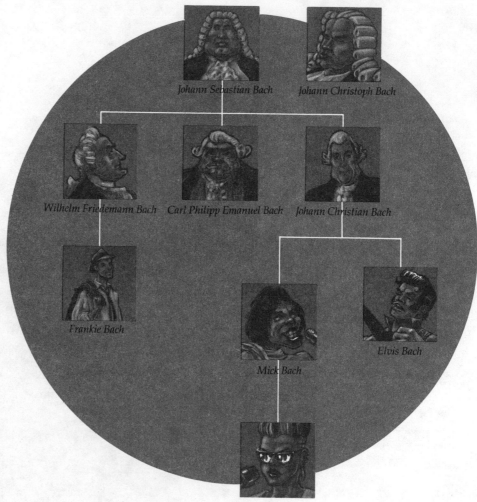

Johann Sebastian Bach

Johann Christoph Bach

Wilhelm Friedemann Bach

Carl Philipp Emanuel Bach

Johann Christian Bach

Frankie Bach

Mick Bach

Elvis Bach

Moon Unit Bach

USIC HAS BEEN CALLED "THE UNIVERSAL LANGUAGE"
—even though it is neither universal nor a language. If you
disagree, try telling an Eskimo that his pants are on fire using
only a kazoo.

Primitive man made the first music by beating on hollow
logs or his enemies' heads, probably in order to drive away evil
spirits. Unfortunately it didn't work and evil spirits remain
plentiful to this day. But music survived nevertheless, because
of its emotional power—power to touch our feelings, to annoy
our parents, to sell soap, to demonstrate our new stereo system, to cover up that embarrassing silence in the elevator.

Musical Notation

In the Middle Ages, singers needed a way to record their chants. Since the recorder had not yet been invented, they wrote them down like this:

nostril·domino·hibiscus·in·alkaseltzer

The notes they used were square, in keeping with the music. Today we use almost the same system, with some additional symbols.

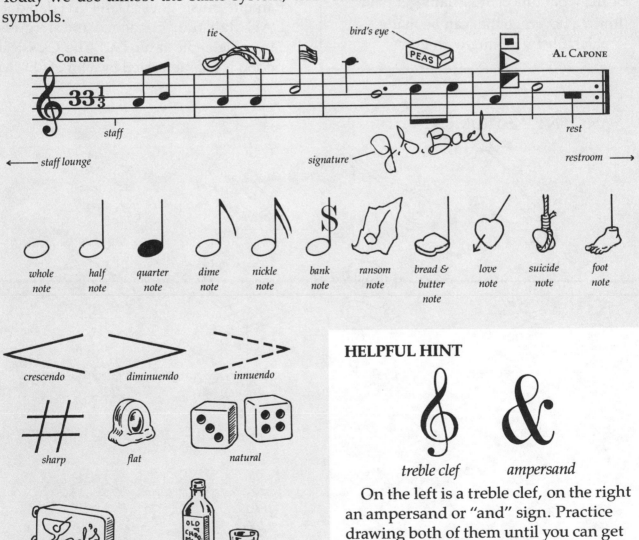

HELPFUL HINT

treble clef   ampersand

On the left is a treble clef, on the right an ampersand or "and" sign. Practice drawing both of them until you can get the little squiggles going the right way *every time*.

23

Music Through the Ages

The history of Western music is one of change. As Plato observed (*Laws*, book VII): "This music the kids listen to now is just a bunch of damn noise. Not like in our day. Hah." In the Middle Ages, simple monophonic music gradually developed into the more complex polyphonic music, through the intermediate stage of stereophonic music. Thus the plainchant of Gregory's time was replaced by chocolatechant, strawberrychant, and mochamintswirlchant.

The progress of musical structure through the development of counterpoint, chromaticism, etc., is a difficult subject. You only need remember a few principles. Baroque music goes "Dah DAH dah dah DAH dah dah"; Rococo music goes "Tweedle-eedle ta ta TA." The Classical period is characterized by a lot of "DUM

TERMS TO REMEMBER

Operetta: a person who helps you make a phone call

Perfect pitch: between the knees and the numbers, and inside the box

Scale: what union musicians get paid

Tonic: a beverage that can be made palatable by mixing with gin

---

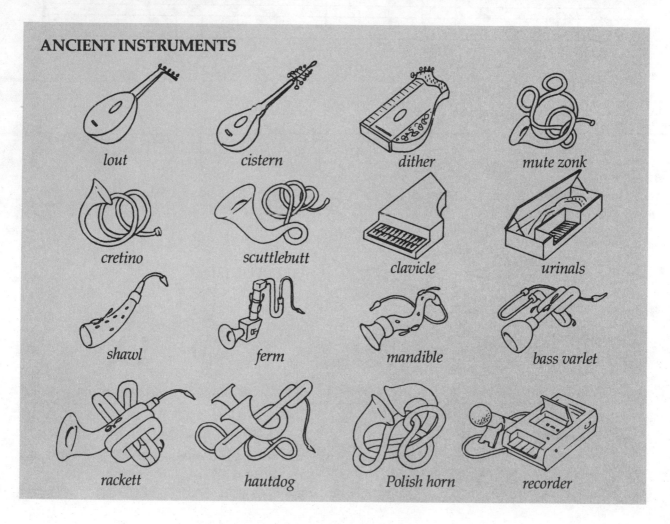

ANCIENT INSTRUMENTS

lout   cistern   dither   mute zonk

cretino   scuttlebutt   clavicle   urinals

shawl   ferm   mandible   bass varlet

rackett   hautdog   Polish horn   recorder

THE MODERN ORCHESTRA

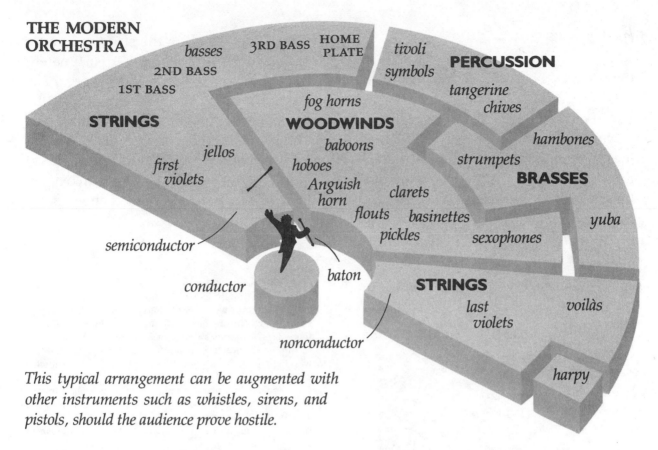

basses
2ND BASS
1ST BASS
3RD BASS
HOME PLATE
tivoli
symbols
PERCUSSION
tangerine
chives
fog horns
STRINGS
WOODWINDS
hambones
jellos
baboons
strumpets
first violets
hoboes
Anguish horn
clarets
BRASSES
flouts
basinettes
yuba
pickles
sexophones
semiconductor
baton
conductor
STRINGS
last violets
voilàs
nonconductor
harpy

This typical arrangement can be augmented with other instruments such as whistles, sirens, and pistols, should the audience prove hostile.

dum diddle diddle DUM" stuff, while Romantic music goes "La-a-a LA-A-A-A la-a-a la-a-a-a-a-a-a."

The orchestra developed over the years as well. The instruments used in Elizabethan music were few and tended to sound like they came from the K-Mart toy section. Later orchestras grew in size, reaching a peak with the Wagnerian orchestra, which often had its own fire department and post office.

Instrumentation grew more diverse and sometimes included such exotica as cannons, as in Tchaikovsky's *1812 Overture*. This famous piece, a failure in its early performances, only achieved popularity after orchestras discovered the trick of using blanks.

MUSIC TRIVIA

Many famous compositions were originally known by other names, often relating to now-forgotten operas and the like. Occasionally even today these old titles are used on obscure record jackets and little-known radio stations.

FAMILIAR TITLE	ORIGINAL TITLE
Lone Ranger Overture	*William Tell Overture*, Rossini
Flash Gordon Suite	*Les Preludes*, Liszt
Theme from *Elvira Madigan*	Piano Concerto No. 21, Mozart
Sergeant Preston of the Yukon Concerto	*Donna Diana Overture*, Reznicek
2001: A Space Odyssey	*Also Sprach Zarathustra*, Strauss
"Helicopter Music" from *Apocalypse Now*	"Ride of the Valkyries" from *Die Walküre*, Wagner
"Here Comes the Bride"	"Wedding March" from *Lohengrin*, Wagner
Captain Video Overture	*Flying Dutchman Overture*, Wagner
Marche Alfred Hitchcock	*Funeral March of a Marionette*, Gounod

The Opera

Opera was born when music joined forces with a powerful new element: fat people bellowing in a foreign language. This combination, along with the ticket prices, has made opera a cvltvral watershed — separating the mere pretenders from the truly pretentious.

Many would-be opera buffs fear that the language barrier will prevent them from understanding the story or **libretto** (Italian for "ridiculous book"). Fortunately, the handy synopses provided here make it easy to enjoy opera. Merely take this volume with you to the performance, plus a small flashlight, and follow along.

Also recommended are supplies of food and water for several days, and an oxygen mask if you have purchased cheap seats in the upper balconies.

HYDROX ET OREO
Christoph Willibald von Gummybear
1762

Hydrox is an example of the **opera boffo**, so called because these works were very popular at the box office.

Act I
Scene: An Idyllic Hillside

Hydrox, a simple shepherd lad, sings of his love for the shepherdess Oreo. Oreo appears, tripping gaily over the hillside. Hydrox helps her up, and they sing a touching duet.

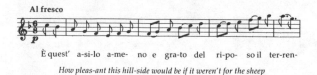

Al fresco

È quest' a-si-lo a-me- no e gra-to del ri-po- so il ter-ren-

How pleas-ant this hill-side would be if it weren't for the sheep

Suddenly a gang of pirates appears and abducts Oreo. Hydrox, in despair, vows to seek the help of the god Mars in rescuing his lost love.

Act II
Scene: The Temple of Mars

Mars agrees to help the grieving youth, but first he must demonstrate that his love is true. He must travel to distant Magnesia and return with a bottle of the magical milk that is found only there.

Act III
Scene: The Seacoast of Magnesia

During the intermission, Hydrox has been shipwrecked and cast ashore, saved only by clutching the bottle of magical milk. As he bemoans his plight in the aria *Un bel di* ("One of those days"), another ship is wrecked and a band of pirates is cast up on the beach. Hydrox recognizes the pirate chieftain who kidnapped his love; he is near death. Putting aside his hatred, he revives the pirate with the magic milk. Suddenly Oreo appears in a blaze of light, transformed; she explains that she is actually the goddess Uno, who had been disguised as a simple peasant girl. To reward Hydrox for his virtue, she transforms him into an end table. As the pirates begin to dance, the curtain falls.

L'ITALIANA IN YUBA CITY
Gioacchino Canelloni
1813

A one-act comic opera in the **mal canto** style.

Scene: A Remote Village in America

Pancetta, a beautiful Italian girl, is touring distant and exotic Yuba City. As she strolls through the bustling marketplace, Mustafa, a young hassock merchant, urges her to buy his wares. Struck by her charms, he sings the playful *Ch'ella mi creda libero* ("Easy credit terms"). As they haggle they are observed by MacSmith, Grand Vizier of the Elks club, who is also smitten by the girl's beauty. The lecherous MacSmith causes her to be seized and transported to his harem. Mustafa appears below her window and vows to rescue her, pledging his love in the plaintive *Vissi d'arte* ("You call this art?"). Pancetta resists MacSmith's lustful advances, and the enraged Vizier has her sold into slavery. On the auction block, she sings longingly of her lost homeland:

Di Pro-ven-za il mar, il suol chi dal cor ti can-cel-lo

I left my heart in San Fran-cis-co

She is purchased by a mysterious Signore Fresno, who, as she beweeps her fate, reveals himself to be Mustafa in disguise. Overjoyed, Pancetta reveals herself to be the wealthy Countess of Magnesia in disguise. A chorus of Elks reveals that Yuba City is actually Napoli in disguise. The curtain falls and the house lights come up, revealing that the audience has gone home.

DAS VOLKSWAGEN
Richard Sauerkraut
1845

An example of the **music drama**, so called because it cannot properly be described as either musical or dramatic.

Act I
Scene 1: A Grotto

In a dank cavern that houses the forge of the gods lives the young hero Eggfried; his brothers Siegfried, a dwarf, Siegmund, a giant, and Siegheil, a toad; and their father and mother, Siegar, a dragon, and Siegarette, an end table. Eggfried rails against having to hang around the grotto with such a peculiar family when he should be out doing heroic deeds. Stealing Siegmund's enchanted bicycle, he defies his father and uses the magic anvil of the gods to forge a sword from it. While he is at it he forges a check on his father's bank account. He names the sword Nothing and sets out into the forest. In a rage, Siegmund invents psychiatry.

Scene 2: The Forest

After tripping over a magic rock, Eggfried discovers that he can understand the language of the birds. He asks a little bird how he may become a great hero. The bird warns him that it will require many hours of singing to very slow music. He vows his willingness and the bird directs him to the nearest dragon. He cleverly tricks the dragon into changing itself into a gerbil, but before he can steal its hoard of gold, it tricks him by changing into a music critic and lambasting his *portamento*. Eggfried flees, reeling from the attack.

Act II
Scene 1: Before the Hall of the Giblets

Eggfried, wandering in a daze, encounters Dristan, king of the Giblets, and his attendants. Eggfried is immediately attracted to Fatlinde, the king's daughter. He has never seen a woman before (except for his mother who, after all, was an end table), but instinctively recognizes that Fatlinde is different by the delicacy of her moustache. When he learns that they are on their way to a song festival, he is excited: here is a way to win Fatlinde's heart. "Take me to your lieder!" he cries.

Scene 2: The Hall of Song

Eggfried enters the singing contest but causes a scandal when he sings the dirty lyrics to "Louie, Louie." The knights advance on him, swords drawn, but Fatlinde intercedes; Eggfried may redeem himself, she says, if he will go to the pope in Rome and ask for his absolution, or at least his autograph. Crushed, Eggfried sets out.

Act III
Prelude

The Prelude begins softly with a restatement of the motive of Eggfried's Ineptitude:

interwoven with that of the Tedium motive:

Slowly the themes of the Sword, Deliverance Through Love, and Dental Hygiene begin to swirl around them, representing Eggfried's confused state of mind. Five insistent notes of the guitar lead of "Louie, Louie" repeatedly interrupt the chaos:

Finally, in a foreshadowing of the catastrophe to come, Sauerkraut's score calls for all the opera's 352 motives to sound at once. The orchestra being inadequate to the task, it is necessary for a section of the audience to be given kazoos and pressed into service.

Scene 1: The Banks of the Rhine

Amid a withered and brown landscape, Fatlinde and her ladies are spinning. When they come to a stop, they see a strange figure floating down the river in a rear engine, air-cooled swan boat. The boat stops and a weary and desolate Eggfried alights. The pope was out to lunch, so his pilgrimage was a failure; he had been able to get a discount swan-boat fare for the return trip. Fatlinde tells him that a curse came upon the land when he left, and she herself has a hangnail that will not heal. She says that she will be his if he renounces his lust for treasure and saturated fats. At that, Eggfried flings Nothing into the waters of the Rhine. Miraculously it reverts to its original state and emerges from the river as a bicycle, ridden by the pope. A great crack opens in the earth and the two lovers plunge into the smoking crevasse. The Rhine overflows; Valhalla crumbles; Krakatoa erupts; there is a 100-car pileup on the Autobahn; 5000 red, white, and blue balloons float down from the ceiling; and the opera house is set afire. As the audience flees in terror, the pope circles the now-ruined stage ringing his little bell, while the two transfigured lovers, clasped in each other's arms, rise slowly toward heaven.

UN BALLO IN MASCARA
Giuseppe Calzone
1853

Originally laid in Massachusetts, this historical opera was considered politically dangerous and the censors demanded the setting be changed.

Act I
Scene 1: A Hall in the Palace of the Doge of Venice

In an audience with the Doge, Fiasco, a ruined nobleman, informs the ruler of a plot on his life by his Hessian mercenaries. In return for this favor he seeks the marriage of his daughter, Albania, to the Doge. The Doge agrees on the condition that Albania lose forty pounds.

Scene 2: The Grounds Near Hogshead Manor

The lovely Albania is strolling by the carp ponds with her Indian maid, Sacajawea. Sir Ashcroft Woodleigh, a ruined Inca nobleman, rides in from a tiger hunt with one of his retainers. After taking the retainer out of his mouth, he passionately embraces Albania and she tearfully informs her of her father's determination to marry her to the Doge. The horrified Sir Ashcroft reveals that he must leave in the morning to accompany Richard the Lion-Hearted on the Second Crusade. The unhappy lovers sing the pitiful *Che gelida manina* ("Hand me that gelato, Che"), then part.

Act II
Scene 1: A Gypsy Encampment on the Banks of the Amazon

As the gaily attired Gypsies square-dance, the vivacious Mitzi sings of the Gypsies' coming traditional festival in *Questo o quello* ("Trick or treat"). Rotundo, her hot-blooded lover, accuses her of unfaithfulness. In an exchange of heated words, Rotundo reveals that Mitzi is actually the daughter of Vasco da Gama and Cher, kidnapped by pirates at an early age, sold into slavery, and finally stolen by the Gypsies. Suddenly, the tense scene is interrupted by the failure of an offstage trumpet to blow on cue. The soldiers of Otto of Burgundy march in singing of their hatred for the Doge:

Del-le fa-ci fes-tan-ti al bar-lu-me

Get a-long, lit-tle Doge

As Oliver Cromwell, leader of the Burgundians, rallies the Gypsies to his cause, Rotundo is kidnapped by some passing pirates. Mitzi, resolved to discover the truth about her birth, disguises herself as an end table and sets sail for Louisiana.

Scene 2: A Tavern in the Swiss Alps

Fiasco, with his two Nubian slaves, has stopped at an inn on the way to Seville where he hopes to enlist the aid of the King of Magnesia. As they drink and make merry, Fiasco sings the roistering *La Donna e Mobile* ("The Lady from Mobile"). Mitzi's ship has stopped in Switzerland on its way to Louisiana; her disguise as an end table enables her to overhear Fiasco's plot.

Act III
Scene 1: The Battlements of Elsinore

A grand ball is underway when a messenger arrives from the front. Albania falls in a faint when she learns that Sir Ashcroft has been killed in battle and her application to Harvard Law School has been rejected. Her father attempts to revive her, singing the aria *Recondita armonia* ("Where's the ammonia?"). The Burgundian ambassador arrives to sue for peace, but the jury only awards him damages and court costs.

Scene 2: A Secret Chamber Beneath the Great Pyramid

As the Doge, Sacajawea, and a character from an entirely different opera hide behind the arras, they observe Albania wandering in her nightgown. The terrible news has driven her mad; in her famous aria she imagines that she is trapped in a long, incomprehensible story.

Scene 3: A Rocky Promontory

Rotundo, having been shipwrecked on the nearby seacoast, discovers the lifeless body of Albania. She has killed herself by sitting under a poisonous tree, common in those parts. Recognizing the locket she wears, he realizes that she is half-sister to Mitzi, cousin to the Doge, and knew someone who once met Don Johnson. As he cradles her in his arms, struck by her beauty, he sings the lengthy *Addio, addio, addio* ("Farewell, farewell, farewell"). Fiasco, the Doge, and the forces of the Holy Inquisition arrive. When Rotundo explains what he has learned, Fiasco orders the Doge seized. Mitzi suddenly throws off her disguise; when she explains what she has learned, the Doge orders Fiasco seized. The Grand Inquisitioner, as confused as the audience, orders everybody seized. As Fiasco, for no particular reason, cries, "Justice is avenged!" the curtain falls.

ALEXANDER PESKY
Modest Stolichnaya
1874

Based on Pushpin's historical drama, this work is now performed in a rewritten version. Stolichnaya, having little training in composition, wrote his original score in crayon.

Act I
Scene 1: A Square in Moscow

It is a melancholy time for Russia. The beloved Czar Boris has died, and the peasants crowd the square. "Alas," cries old Pyotr Pyotrvich Pyutrid, "the Tzar gave us a crust of bread a week to live on, had us beaten every day, and ate our children for dinner. Where will we find another ruler so enlightened?" The peasants murmur their agreement; even the secret police are moved by the people's sorrow, and nod sympathetically as they bludgeon them to the ground. The bells of the city begin to toll and Prince Turnoff appears. He announces that the young Czarevich Alexander has accepted the crown. The peasants cheer joyously, then die of starvation.

Scene 2: The Apartments of the Csar in the Kremlin

The young Tsar is in a cheerful mood, happily pulling the wings off bluebirds. Prince Turnoff warns him that he faces many troubles in his reign. But Alexander's thoughts are of his betrothed, Princess Samovar. Suddenly a messenger brings word that the Princess has been eaten by a passing wolf while in church. Devastated, Alexander orders ten thousand peasants shot in remembrance.

Act II
Scene 1: An Encampment on the Steppes

It is a melancholy time for Russia. The peasants are starving, the crops have failed, and happy hour has been reduced to three minutes. Dimwitri, the pretender to the throne, has raised an army of Cossacks disguised in cassocks. He relates his plan to march on Moscow, confront the Czar, and see who can hit the lowest note.

Scene 2: The Throne Room in the Kremlin

Alexander has summoned the boyars to advise him. "The peasants are revolting," says their leader, Slivovitz. "Don't give me straight lines," replies Alexander. "Give me advice." Chastened, the boyars depart to go look for girlars.

Act III
Scene: The Hall of the Duma

It is still a melancholy time for Russia. The peasants are still starving, the crops have failed again, and summer reruns have started. The Duma is thronged as the people await the expected invasion. Prince Turnoff arrives with word that the pretender has tripped while coming down the Steppes; the revolt has failed. The people cheer as the bells gaily ring. Suddenly word arrives that the Ksar has been eaten by a wolf in his apartments. The peasants bemoan their tragic fate. "After the revolution," warns old Pyotr Pyotrvich threateningly, "everyone will be eaten by wolves, not just the rich and powerful." As the bells toll mournfully, the curtain falls.

GOLDILOCKEN UND DIE DREI BÄREN
Engelbert Pumpernickle
1893

Short operas such as this were performed between the acts of longer works, often in the snack bar.

Act I
Scene: A Clearing in the Forest

The curtain rises on Goldilocken, lost and alone. She sings of the treachery of the Duke of Brabant, who has murdered her mother, father, and poodle Heinrich, and forced her to flee for her life into the woods. Weary, she lies down to sleep, singing:

Lentil

Dann wach-en auf die Ster-ne

I won-der where the chor-us and bal-let are

As she sleeps, the Virgin Mary appears accompanied by two hundred angels and sings her blessing on the innocent child. The angels dance, then all depart. Goldilocken is awakened by the first drops of an approaching storm.

Entr'acte

Before the curtain, Goldilocken flees the raging tempest, as the orchestra plays the "Storm Music"; furious cymbal crashes suggest lightning bolts, while thunder is represented by the noise of stagehands changing the set.

Act II
Scene: The House of the Three Bears

Goldilocken has found refuge in a deserted house and has eaten some porridge she found there. Startled by the sound of someone arriving, she hides. The three bears enter and sing the renowned trio ("The Porridge Song"). They are interrupted by the arrival of the Duke of Brabant and his troops. He commands the bears' suits to be stripped off, and they are revealed as Goldilocken's mother and father and poodle Heinrich—not dead after all, but hiding in the forest disguised as bears. Overjoyed at finding her family alive, Goldilocken rushes forth to embrace them. "Aha," snarls the evil Duke, "You shall die, too!" But Mama Bear points out the locket that Goldilocken wears around her neck, proving that she is actually the Duke's long-lost sister. Stricken with remorse, the Duke reveals that the porridge was poisoned. Goldilocken dies, but not before forgiving the Duke for his evil ways. Drawing his sword, Papa Bear falls on the Duke and in the struggle, both are killed. Mama Bear, driven mad, throws herself out the window to her death. As the troops acclaim him, Heinrich seizes the throne of Magnesia.

FILET MIGNON
Jules Bassinette
1894

A romantic work in the **tourismo** style, showing opera's increasing tendency toward realism.

Act I
Scene: A Drawing Room in Paris

Filet Mignon, the toast of Paris, is giving a gala ball at her home. Filet and her guests sing the famous "Drinking Song," in which they remind the audience that drinks are served during intermissions and that the bar revenue is all that supports the opera house. After the guests leave, her wealthy patron and lover, Monsieur Étouffée, enters waving a handful of bills. "Look at the size of these sets," he cries. "I can't afford this extravagance any longer!" She resolves to find a new patron, even if it means getting government support. The handsome young Framboise enters and sings of his love for her. Coughing lyrically, she explains that their love is hopeless as she has a terrible wasting disease. Framboise claims that it does not matter to him; she can afford to lose a few pounds anyway.

Act II
Scene: Filet's House in the Country

Filet and Framboise are living in the country, where they can get by with a smaller cast. The elder Rémoulade, Framboise's father, enters. He urges her to leave Framboise, as her taste for pasta and expensive productions will ruin his son's chances in show business. Sadly she agrees and departs. Framboise returns from his acting lesson and discovers to his horror that Filet has gone. His father explains that a few short years of happiness is the most anyone can hope for, especially a tenor. Distraught, Framboise pulls a pistol from his pocket and shoots himself. He is, however, only wounded, and is able to sing for another twenty minutes.

Act III
Scene: A Wretched Garret

Filet is on her deathbed. Ravaged by her disease, she has dwindled to a mere two-ninety. The doctor sadly affirms that her disease is fatal. "If only she could have gotten that NEA grant," he says. Deeply touched, the elder Rémoulade sings *Adieu, adieu, adieu* ("Farewell, farewell, farewell"). Filet attempts to sing, but cannot. Dramatically, she speaks her final words, "Melody . . . melody . . . I have run out of melody!" and dies. Framboise enters, having rushed to Paris from Hollywood where he had gotten a job in the movies. Alas, he is too late. He sinks to the floor weeping as the curtain falls and the opera house is torn down for a parking lot.

PETER GRIM
Benjamin Bitter
1937

This modern classic is included in most companies' repertoires to provide a respite from the rigors of performing before an audience.

Act I
Scene: A Prison Cell

The curtain rises on a brutal, discordant note from the full orchestra, which is sustained throughout the performance. Peter Grim, dressed in gray rags, lies in his gray, filthy prison cell. He sings of the cruel fate that has kept him imprisoned these nineteen years for a parking violation he did not commit. He recalls the village of his birth and his sweetheart, Griselda, whom he worshipped from afar but never actually met, and who is now dead. He concludes that he's not much worse off now.

Act II
Scene: A Town Square

In the gray, filthy Welsh linoleum-mining village of St. Dismal, the townspeople, dressed in gray rags, sing of how wretched and starving they are. Edna, daughter of Griselda and of the brutal miner whom she married and who murdered her before himself drowning, tells of how she wishes her mother had actually met Peter Grim, who loved her. She wouldn't have been any better off, she says, but at least the story might have had a point. She commits suicide by throwing herself into the town well.

Act III
Scene: A Prison Cell

The action of Act III is much the same as that of Act I.

Act IV
Scene: A Town Square

A series of disasters have befallen St. Dismal. The linoleum mine has caved in, the church has collapsed during the memorial service, and the well water has become undrinkable. The surviving townspeople are whipped into a rage at their plight by Dick, a socialist agitator. They rush into the auditorium, throttling and cudgeling any remaining members of the audience they can find, shouting "Bourgeois dogs!" and the like.

Act V
Scene: A Prison Cell

In his cell, Peter is briefly heartened by a rumor that there is to be an amnesty and he will be able to return to his village. Then word arrives that St. Dismal has been obliterated by a mudslide. Grim reflects bitterly on the tragic irony of it. The rumor of amnesty proves to be false. Aware that he is dying of scurvy, he sings the aria *Goodbye, goodbye, goodbye* ("Farewell, farewell, farewell"), which, poignantly, almost achieves melody. He dies as the filthy gray curtain falls.

Recent trends are toward a more popular approach to opera productions, as this poster shows.

The Dance

The dance offers the perfect combination of the art of music, the beauty of the human body in movement, and a way to get out of Russia (classically known as the *tour de la défection*).

The mastery of flawlessly executed *battlements* and *entremets* does not come easily. The would-be dancer must train rigorously from an early age — preferably beginning before birth. The novice thoroughly studies the five positions and the basic movements before attempting the more advanced *fondue*, *pomme de terre*, and *croissant au beurre*.

CORPSE DE BALLET: Mme. Samovara's tragic mishap during a performance of La Fille Mal Dansée.

1st position

2nd position

3rd position

4th position

5th position

jeté

sauté

32

Despite this exhaustive training, the vast majority of ballerinas fail because they turn out to be too tall, too short, undertrained, overtrained, or are run over by a train.

A $$$-SAVING TIP

Thrifty cvltvre fans might consider attending the opera rather than the ballet. At the opera they usually have a ballet, too, but at the ballet they never have an opera.

à plat

bandagio

A classic example of the German ballet, Beethoven's Return of the Creatures of Prometheus. *Inset: Gerda Schnitzel displays her famous* embonpoint.

Recommended Recordings

These compositions may be considered basic to a well-rounded, impressive-looking record collection. The recorded versions cited here are outstanding for interpretation, fidelity, or the pretty picture on the cover. Many are also available in the new CD format, which has less surface noise, longer life, and higher interest rates, although there is a substantial penalty for early withdrawal.

Bach, THE ILL-TEMPERED COMPOSER
Rearguard BG-10478
Claudio Rrrowrr, pianist

Beethoven, "EROTICA" SYMPHONY
Telephon 1147 639
Amsterdam Concertgoboom Orchestra
Bernard Hijinks, conductor

Beethoven, INFIDELIO
Argive 647801
Chorus and Orchestra of the Vienna State Opera for the Criminally Insane
Karl Rictus, conductor

Debussy, LA MERDE
Nosuch H-455
Academy of Prince Albert-in-the-Can
Sir Colin Divot, conductor

Gershwin, RHAPSODY IN PUCE
Odium 199
MTV Symphony Orchestra
Leonard Sideburns, conductor

Liszt, LES QUAALUDES
Angle DS 144356
Orchestre de la Suisse Watch
Karl Boom, conductor

Mendelssohn, ACCIDENTAL MUSIC TO A MIDSUMMER NIGHT'S DREAM
Capitalist 3777
Bathroom Festival Orchestra
Daniel Barenboom, conductor

Mendelssohn, PEACE MARCH OF THE PRIESTS
Deutsche Gestalt Gemütlichkeit 3330 676
Stuttgart Chamber of Commerce Orchestra
Raymond Leper, conductor

Mozart, THE MAGIC SLATE
Argyle ML 34277
Chorus and Orchestra of the Royal Opera House, Covert Garden
Sir Adrian Dolt, conductor

Mussorgsky, PICTURES OF AN EXHIBITIONIST
Oddity 32 733933
Cleveland Sympathy Orchestra
Ricardo Mutant, conductor

Offenbach, ORPHEUS IN HIS UNDERWEAR
Erratum STU 77080
Boomberg Symphony Orchestra
Loren Mazeltov, conductor

Orff, CARMINA PIRANHA
Megaphon 3455 33
Academy of St. Christopher-on-the-Dashboard
Neville Marinara, conductor
With the Hangover Boys' Choir

Prokofiev, PETER AND THE IMPERIALIST
Turnover TVA 72333
Eastman Kodak Symphony Orchestra
Howard Handsome, conductor

Purcell, TRUMPET INVOLUNTARY
Serigraph S 52222
Disneyland Wind Ensemble
Sir Thomas Beechnut, conductor

Respighi, ANCIENT ERRORS AND DUNCES FOR THE LOUT
Telefunky CX3 42256
I Solisti di Milpitas

Respighi, THE PINES OF YUBA CITY
Archaic DT 347631
Halley's Comet Orchestra
Sir John Barbarian, conductor

Rimsky-Korsakov, LE COQ AU VIN
Turnoff TWA 503477
Vienna Volkswagen Orchestra
Richard Boinggg, conductor

Schubert, "UNFURNISHED" SYMPHONY
Deutsche Gewurztraminer Gazelleschlag 8988 646
New York Philanthropic Orchestra
Ernest Answerman, conductor

Smetana, THE BATTERED BRIDE
Argot ZPG 122
Barbarian Radio Orchestra
Hans Upp, conductor

Stravinsky, THE FIREBUG
CPA 23334
Glamoureax Orchestra of Paris
Pierre Boulangerie, conductor

Tacobell, CANNON
Megaphon 2221 565
English Chamberpot Orchestra
Claudio Abbadabba, conductor

Tchaikovsky, MARCHE SLOB
His Master's Vice ASD 1342
London Pandemonic Orchestra
Michael Teeter Totter, conductor

Verdi, THE SICILIAN VESPAS
Gummed Label GL 95340
Royal Pain Philharmonic Orchestra
Carl and Maria Giulini, conductors

THREE COMPOSERS WHOSE NAMES YOU CAN TEACH YOUR DOG

1. Bach
2. Orff
3. Bartók

THREE COMPOSERS WHOSE NAMES YOU CAN TEACH YOUR CAT

1. Milhaud
2. Glière
3. Auber

III. The Visual Arts

Vita brevis est, ars longa.
(Art is cheap, but framing is expensive.)
　　—SENECA

The Elgin Marbles

THE VISUAL ARTS—painting and sculpture—have long been regarded as the highest expression of man's aspirations, emotions, and skill. Today they are a smart investment opportunity as well.

Paintings are generally used to cover cracks in walls. You can find a canvas—or, if you prefer, velvet—to harmonize with any décor.

Sculptures are what you bump into when you step back to look at a painting. They often double as elegant lamps or planters.

In either case, they are a blue-chip hedge against inflation. The public has learned its lesson from those avant-garde nineteenth-century artists who starved in obscurity, and whose works later sold for megabucks. It now understands that *any* art—no matter how radical, offensive, or hideous—is a potential big money-maker.

The contemporary museum vividly demonstrates that art has become cvltvre's growth industry. The art museum of old was a drab, dusty place patronized by a handful of esthetes. Today, a visit to a museum—with its blockbuster shows, crowds, lavish installations, and souvenir shops—is more like a visit to an elegant shopping mall.

Gala opening at the Metropolitan Gift Shop and Museum of Art, New York

36

Restoration

Restoration and preservation of art is one of a museum's major responsibilities. Many works, especially sculptures from classical antiquity, have suffered from erroneous attempts at reconstruction. Others remain in a fragmentary state.

The recent discovery of the so-called "Valley of the Noses" at Bubopolis (the modern Yuba City) should change all that. Workmen there accidentally uncovered an underground cache of 13,000 noses, mostly in marble, from the classical period. Also found in the chamber were 9000 arms, 7000 legs, and 4000 male members. Restorers will be kept busy for years to come by the find.

PORTRAIT BUST OF THE EMPEROR DETRITUS
2nd century AD
This restoration is now thought to be incorrect; the toga is in the wrong style for the period.

X-ray photography is one of the modern expert's tools. Rembrandt's clients complained that the original version of The Night Watch *was "too dark"; he was compelled to repaint it. X-rays reveal the first version beneath the repainting.*

Former incorrect restoration of the Laocoon *and corrected version*

The Artist's Techniques

In learning his complex craft, the artist must master color, perspective, the proportions of the human body, and getting the cap off the tube of paint.

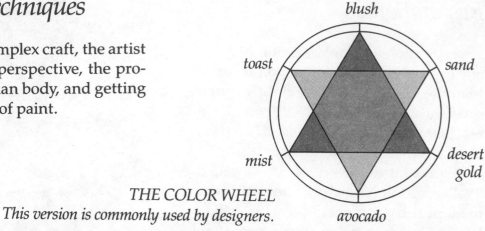

THE COLOR WHEEL
This version is commonly used by designers.

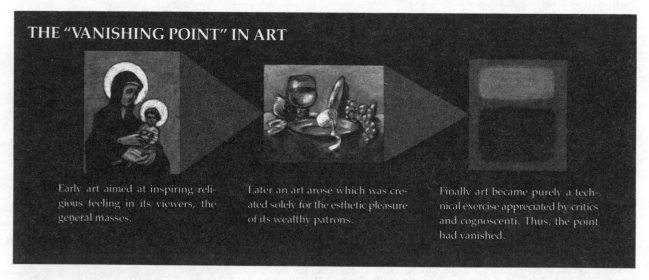

THE "VANISHING POINT" IN ART

Early art aimed at inspiring religious feeling in its viewers, the general masses.

Later an art arose which was created solely for the esthetic pleasure of its wealthy patrons.

Finally art became purely a technical exercise appreciated by critics and cognoscenti. Thus, the point had vanished.

In preparing a painting, an artist first makes a sketch called a **cartoon.**

THE IDEALIZED HUMAN FIGURE

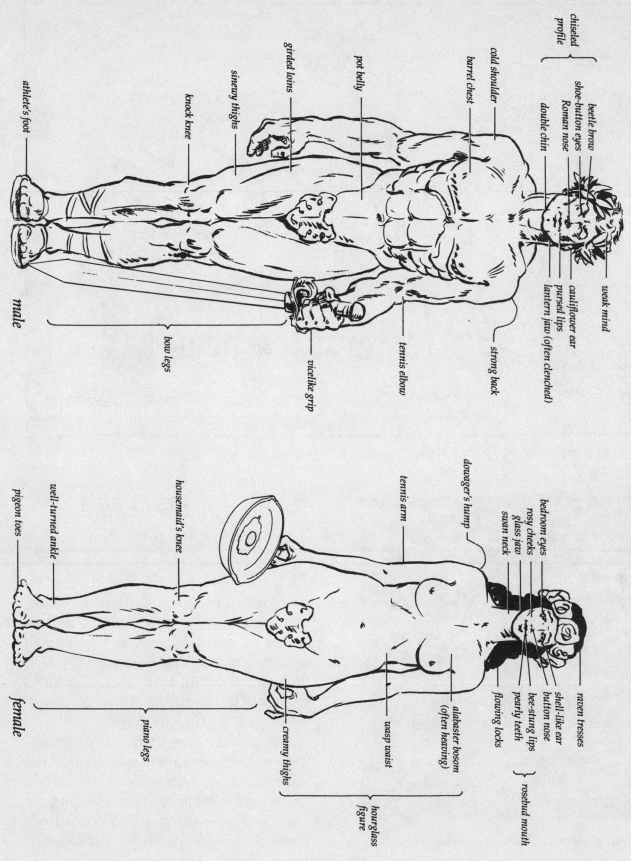

male

chiseled profile
beetle brow
shoe-button eyes
Roman nose
double chin
cold shoulder
barrel chest
girded loins
pot belly
sinewy thighs
knock knee
athlete's foot
weak mind
cauliflower ear
pursed lips
lantern jaw (often clenched)
strong back
tennis elbow
vicelike grip
bow legs

female

dowager's hump
bedroom eyes
rosy cheeks
glass jaw
swan neck
tennis arm
housemaid's knee
well-turned ankle
pigeon toes
raven tresses
shell-like ear
button nose
bee-stung lips
pearly teeth
flowing locks
rosebud mouth
alabaster bosom (often heaving)
wasp waist
creamy thighs
hourglass figure
piano legs

Anonymous, 15th century, Death and the Anchorman, *cheese engraving*

El Greco, View of Toledo, *gauche*

Painting and Sculpture Through the Ages

Classical Greek art is characterized by harmony of proportion, spiritual grace, and missing parts. The Greek sculptors employed marble to attain a quality of solidity and weight in their works, which they hoped would make them harder to steal. It didn't work and in the nineteenth century Greece lost its marbles.

The greatest Greek artist was Epidermis, whose monumental frieze for the Temple of Uno, completed in 96 BC, was known as the Big Frieze of '96. Other great works of antiquity are Perphidias's inventive *Hinged Victory*, Crouton's tur-

40

Copley, Spielberg and the Shark
oil on troubled waters

bulent and dynamic *Hector and Achilles at Jazzercise Class,* and the famous bust of a man's head by Anopheles (now missing one ear) known as the *Vincent de Milo.*

The Romans took over the subjects and techniques of Greek art by the simple expedient of taking over Greece.

With the coming of the Middle Ages, art was dominated by religious themes. Characteristic of this period are a creative approach to anatomy, the invention of the halo, and no naked people.

The Renaissance saw a rebirth of classical technique. This is the period of such

David, Death of Marat
felt-tip on Masonite

FAKES

Fraudulent works of art abound. The well-known bronze horse shown here deceived scholars at a famous museum for years. To avoid being "burned" yourself, remember these pointers:

- Be suspicious of "Old Masters" offered for sale at gas stations.
- Think twice about paintings in frames made from gilded macaroni.
- Check that the artist's signature is spelled correctly. These are typical forgers' errors: *Piccaso Rembrant ·Da Vinchi·*

masterworks as Leonardo's *Virgin on the Rocks* and Michelangelo's *David* (known familiarly to art scholars as "Mike's *Dave*"). It was Michelangelo who endured the extreme hardships of painting the ceiling of the Sistine Chapel. The worst part was that the pope would come around every day, point, and yell up, "You missed a spot." Major works from this period are Vermicelli's *The Three Disgraces* and Tofutti's *Last Tupperware Party*.

In the north, the Renaissance produced the *Barbecue of the Lapiths and Centaurs* by Führer, and Van Duck's *Jacob and Esau on Old MacDonald's Farm*.

The seventeenth and eighteenth centuries saw the growth of extreme and mannered styles, as represented by the swirling and overwrought compositions of Peter Paul Mounds, best known for his *Hannibal Crossing the Street*. Major works are Van Der Vander's *Marius Amid the Ruins of Yuba City* and Sir Thomas Easel's *Mrs. Siddons as an End Table*.

Manet
Déjeuner sur l'herbe
(Picnic on the Grass)
detail
crayon on shirt cardboard

Rodin
The Burgers of Calais
lost-tofu casting

Europe's unsettled political state in the early nineteenth century influenced much art, including Croissant's *Napoleon Crossing His Eyes* and Francisco Guacamole's terrifying *Cronos Devouring His Lunch*. A Romantic tendency in painting led to an interest in gruesome or *outré* subjects, typified by the grisly *Raft of the Love Boat*.

But the real break with tradition came with the Impressionists. The art world was shocked by their renditions of Cagney, Bogart, and Karloff. Monet was best known for his Peter Lorre, while Renoir did a dynamite Edward G. Robinson. The Impressionists were forced to open their own gallery, the *Salon de Refuse*, in order to show their paintings and do their routines.

One of the most versatile of the group was Pissarro, who began his unusual career by conquering the Inca empire before turning to painting. Important works of this period are Pissoir's *Pond with Water Lilies*, Bizarro's *Water Lilies with Pond*, and Déglacé's *More Damn Water Lilies*.

In the twentieth century, the role of painting and sculpture was largely supplanted by macramé.

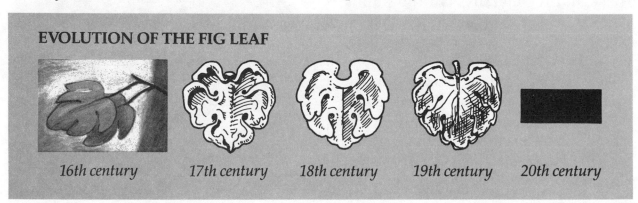

EVOLUTION OF THE FIG LEAF

16th century   *17th century*   *18th century*   *19th century*   *20th century*

Things to Do

Connect the dots to see Seurat's Sunday Afternoon on the Grande Jatte

```
•2085   •2045  •2326   •324    •568   •767  •1223   •954  •1864   •571  •2005   •690 •1838   •221    •413   •48   •2446  •2044  •1642   •981   •628
•722   •1028  •1718  •1228  •2452  •1595  •1841  •1462   •594  •1053   •705   •753  •1941   •783   •2110   •190  •1202   •832   •565  •1508
•2204  •1263   •800  •2152  •2443   •872  •2361  •1212  •1006  •2246  •1632   •1556  •1507  •1746   •1121   •811  •1124  •1983   •376  •1565
•1399   •689   •84   •83   •828   •690   •86   •182  •1715   •531  •2190   •501   •824  •1855  •1830  •2257   •2312   •1544   •323  •2289   •706  •2053
•1222  •2154  •1406   •306   •971   •64   •29   •346  •1646  •1861   •1674   •789   •810  •1709   •469  •2314   •1804  •1838   •316  •2150   •1823   •211
•1242   •33  •2268   •554   •783   •836   •1900  •2235   •811   •202   •1930   •580  •1589   •1088  •2364  •1890   •1897  •2038  •1637  •1073  •1507  •1226
•1190   •171  •1604   •129  •2372   •826  •2409   •612   •458   •2432   •632   •2492   •46   •983   •1435  •2285   •603   •967   •124   •419
•627   •84   •926  •1478  •2201  •1749   •870   •111   •533  •2287   •1288   •439   •951   •985   •2124   •772   •857  •2213  •2409  •2360  •2439   •1355
•1059   •842  •2066  •1019  •2388   •324  •2225   •117  •2493   •2387  •2206  •1041  •1406   •240  •1920  •1087  •1651   •17   •756   •547  •1847  •1594
•1740  •1836  •1030  •1913   •332  •1712  •2227  •1336  •1464   •759   •128  •2435   •1415   •86   •2066   •659   •896  •1185  •1949  •1834  •1613
•151  •1939  •1139  •2063  •1078   •278  •1364   •251   •489   •616  •2475   •2432   •82   •2124   •950  •1354   •1677   •47  •1146  •1616   •1376
•941  •1655  •1191   •107  •1016  •2287  •1809   •213   •676   •526  •2377  •2098   •77   •10   •1421  •2206  •2499   •640  •2047   •444  •1509
•837   •18   •919  •2022   •191  •1724  •1299   •548  •1954  •1514   •617   •593  •1117   •1294  •1095  •2267  •2305   •723  •2167   •800  •1536
•2381  •2201   •1162  •2285   •734  •2373   •81   •773   •632   •219  •2110   •2169   •804  •1735  •1392  •1914  •2218   •726   •318  •2154
•47   •530   •530  •1051  •1448   •545   •450   •378  •1580   •558  •1860  •1899   •253  •1109  •1900   •1296  •1063  •2014  •1318   •600
•1966   •876  •1749   •123  •1098   •560  •1439  •2074  •1935  •1233   •542  •2460   •370  •2177  •1591   •942  •1753  •1979  •2222   •82  •1442  •1676
•2418  •1688   •772   •725   •837  •2452   •231  •1836   •217  •1263  •1321   •20  •1539   •650  •1632   •940   •422  •1421  •1070  •1046
•794  •1626  •2167   •184   •451  •1062  •2078   •806  •2289  •1227  •2450  •1495   •954  •1703  •1695   •1143  •1030   •681   •661  •1062   •260  •1180
•1906   •942   •389   •932  •1644   •985   •826  •2048  •1062   •194  •1268  •1359   •417  •2423   •4   •1230   •440  •1474  •1482  •2107   •770
•4   •614  •1855  •1148   •483   •122  •2299   •131   •343   •620  •1179  •1783   •550   •64  •1165  •1989   •967   •29  •2231   •186  •2208  •1299  •1098
•1173  •1354  •1062  •1462   •821   •617  •1891  •1800   •664   •936  •1682  •1383  •1873  •2041   •2135  •1061  •2142  •2495  •1284   •923
•1446   •673  •1627  •1032  •1330  •1945   •660  •1445  •1778   •511  •2067  •1732  •1761   •236  •2290   •2492  •1930  •2398  •2315  •2034   •301
•2262  •2331   •914  •1433  •1797   •695  •1326   •250  •1258   •49  •2382  •1456  •1300  •419   •638   •811   •317  •1081  •1157  •2311   •955  •1639  •1077
•912   •226  •1957   •771   •855  •2113  •1523  •1829   •574  •1585  •1279  •1630   •386  •2355   •551   •499   •204   •600  •2232   •254   •524   •914   •164
•370   •132  •1271  •2142   •677   •558  •2476  •1952  •1415  •2231   •91   •1520   •70  •1345   •823  •1692   •355  •1413  •1515   •619
•484   •579  •2078  •1386   •545  •1293  •1027  •1716   •254   •363  •2038   •207  •1838  •2200   •1065  •1796   •692  •1227  •1834   •410   •629   •733
•1128  •1566  •1093  •2243   •981   •173  •1022  •1498  •1119   •777   •926   •209  •1872  •2399   •338   •1076  •1704   •400  •1818   •69
•1349   •861  •2089  •1431   •950  •2347   •31   •285   •753   •577  •2237   •162  •2116   •420  •1531  •1934  •1136   •2255   •344  •1304   •522  •1723
•542   •55  •1058   •906   •155  •1361   •451   •314   •222   •262  •1052  •1290   •1739   •1379  •1176  •2004  •2346  •1061   •323  •1768   •338
•2117  •1624   •315  •1759   •231  •2091   •1985  •1546   •658   •960  •1774   •2262   •2397  •1602   •1121  •1947   •78  •1375  •1279   •949
•717  •1480  •1619   •891  •2348  •1094   •522  •1042   •361   •282  •2470   •318  •1795   •529  •2251   •1018  •1089  •2366  •1989   •1583
•1342  •2151  •2441   •773  •1475   •868  •1121  •1331   •279   •1916  •2251   •925   •2091   •687   •56   •1156  •1693  •2270   •427  •2106   •152   •804
•1647   •500   •727  •1068  •2215   •690   •20   •787   •255  •1142  •2099   •1376   •468   •399   •518  •2485  •1176  •2429  •2026  •1429   •1693  •2109
•486   •157   •96   •291   •208   •117    •2141  •2398   •497  •1307   •1855  •2380   •154   •2149   •523  •1660   •26   •863  •1441  •2356
•2234   •127  •1818   •230  •1539  •1488  •1562   •281  •1766  •1602   •616   •70   •620  •1310   •688   •1317   •664   •415  •1284  •2286   •1968
•2013   •539   •540  •1158  •2342  •1054   •2193   •310  •1558   •859   •172  •2288   •2002   •46  •1599   •1196   •858   •786   •774
•1608  •1303  •1722  •1295   •350   •141  •1377   •536  •2312   •862  •1050   •735  •1172   •509   •313   •779   •798   •1503  •1188   •1274   •359   •248
•1186   •133  •1207  •1553   •335  •2495  •2487  •1594  •1157   •361  •1323   •735   •1011  •1634   •356  •2271  •1045   •761  •1364  •2305  •1339   •752
•1572  •1003  •1463  •1373  •1114  •1874  •1882  •1965   •2012   •603  •1128   •1500   •376  •1096   •35   •872  •1548   •750  •1678   •892  •1895
•169   •207  •1384  •2491   •697   •157   •778   •2417   •615  •2407   •1645   •467   •528  •1795  •1513  •1070   •203   •569  •2132  •1868  •2493
•1762  •2151  •1304  •1820  •2082  •2465   •1211  •1525   •44  •2313   •959  •1837   •380   •23  •1412   •377  •1567   •413   •598   •343  •1141  •1547
•533   •403  •2374   •765   •1920   •471   •595  •2192  •2165   •151   •252   •1788   •1074   •241   •966   •484  •2463  •1022  •1061  •2076  •1807   •56  •2358
•1062   •875  •2265   •292   •921   •1961  •2201   •1405   •824  •1269   •774  •1931   •677  •2376  •1364   •391  •2395  •1048  •2095  •1991  •1844
•1268   •156   •776  •1965   •875  •1649  •1736   •596  •1431  •1016   •535  •1770   •1119   •645  •2050   •876   •515   •353  •2061   •590   •400  •1722  •1881
•210   •1327  •1910   •362  •2102   •796  •2180  •1243   •734   •609   •2330  •1049   •117  •2488   •1798   •467   •2347   •21  •2157  •1991  •1001
•1054   •1389   •126  •1881   •819   •1881  •2051  •1313   •11  •1433  •2412   •1780  •1651  •1219   •398   •1504  •1190  •1373  •1246   •750  •1839  •2297
•172   •1020  •1643   •462   •330   •21   •178   •1168  •1315   •565  •2029   •782   •218   •745  •1852   •1142   •185  •2432   •764  •1397   •3
•68   •161   •1432  •1047   •634   •186  •1621  •1839   •2136   •476  •1156   •557   •817  •1034   •1756   •262  •2481   •524  •1075  •1540  •1424   •974
•773  •1314  •1992  •1164  •1703   •2377  •1321   •115  •768  •2476   •1166   •2352  •1132   •919   •2118  •2439  •1451   •549   •649  •2151  •1238   •1132   •854
```

A PROJECT

When we see classical statues, they sometimes look funny because they have blank white eyeballs. In ancient times, these statues usually had the pupils painted in. Try filling in the eyeballs on pictures of old statues in books. There, doesn't that look better?

Take a felt-tip pen with you when you go to the museum, and draw in the eyeballs on the statues there. Watch out for the guards, who are sometimes not as familiar with the principles of classical art as they should be. No cross-eyes, now!

THREE ARTISTS WHOSE NAMES YOU CAN TEACH YOUR DOG

1. Arp
2. Braque
3. Böcklin

THREE ARTISTS WHOSE NAMES YOU CAN TEACH YOUR CAT

1. Rouault
2. Miró
3. Weir

IV. The Wonderful World of Books

A Book of Verses underneath the Bough,
A Loaf of Bread, a Jug of Wine, and, uh,
The Tuna Melt and Side of Fries. Okay,
And what's the lady gonna have today?
    —RUBY AT OMAR KHAYYAM'S HICK'RY PIT

BOOKS ARE LIKE A MAGIC ARROW, an arrow by which poetry, literature, auto repair, indeed all of cvltvre may soar from the minds of the artists and thinkers who created them swiftly to their final target—the remainder bin.

With books, we can travel in outer space, talk to Shakespeare, conquer the world, prop open doors and windows.

In them we can gaze on the faces, and wonder at the thoughts, of people from the remotest times, like in your high school yearbook. Through them, inhabitants of one part of the globe can understand the feelings and customs of those of another far distant, usually resulting in war. Indeed, it is just conceivable that through the unifying power of literature all peoples may yet come to live together as brothers and sisters: in continuous, squabbling enmity.

Literature begins as myth, folktale, and prayer. This traditional Sue Indian prayer is probably typical of the poetry of preliterate peoples:

O sacred sky-bunny
Hayhuh hunnhuh
Bite the noses of my enemies
Hayhuh hunnhuh
As you did in the ancient-time
Before people had knees
And had to walk funny
Clump-clump, clump-clump
Pierce their eyeballs, o sky-bunny
Pierce their eyeballs
Crush their skulls
Oh boy, oh boy
As you did in the ancient-time
When you devoured the hero-gerbil
When you made the sun and moon
From his shoelaces
Hunnhuh hunnhuh
I forget the rest

This powerful poem is an example of the vital contributions of non-European peoples to world cvltvre. Nevertheless, there will be no further mention of non-Western art in this book.

The invention of writing made it possible to preserve and transmit such works to succeeding ages. The first known

Pictographic clay tablet found misfiled at Knish in Hippopotamia, ca. 3500 BC

example of written literature appears to be a prayer of offering to an otherwise unknown goddess, "Urt."

Thirty-three horses
Forty [bushels of] barley
One hundred jars of [. . .] beer
Sixteen(?) oxen
Four hundred silver g[onzagas]
[. . .] Urt: do not let [the] tax collector(?) see this tablet [. . .] show(?) him [the] other ones [. . .].

Such documents only became practical with the development of alphabetic writing systems. Before the alphabet there was of course no alphabetical order; hence any document, once filed, could seldom be found again. Doubtless many great works were lost in this way.

Evolution of the modern alphabet from pictographic writing

NAME	PROTO-SEMANTIC 1600 BC	EARLY VENUSIAN 1100 BC	ARCHAIC GEEK 800 BC	MODERN ALPHABET
tiktakh				A
mirsediz				B
kopirit				C
mikki				M
kommi				R
pyzin				X
cibiyes				⬬

FLORIDA·TAMPA·SECAUCUS·UT·MOBILE·FARGO·VERMONT·
CINCINNATI·MONTANA·ME·TUCUMCARI·DECATUR·
PROVO·VIRGINIA·TEMPE·IN·AUGUSTA·BILOXI·ALBUQUERQUE·
OR·PENSACOLA·DUBUQUE·MIAMI·COLUMBUS·PASADENA·

Earliest manuscript of Vergil's Aeneid, *5th century*

Our written versions of the great Geek epics the *Idiot* and the *Oddity*, are based on an older oral tradition. Scholars agree that the author of these poems, if he ever existed, was mythical.

ANSWERS TO RHETORICAL QUESTIONS IN POETRY

This summary may be helpful to busy poetry fans who don't have time to read the entire work.

Q. Shall I compare thee to a summer's day?
A. No.

Q. Who is Silvia?
A. Daughter of the Duke of Milan, beloved of Valentine.

Q. Why dois your brand sae drop wi' bluid, Edward, Edward?
A. He killed his father.

Q. What is so rare as a day in June?
A. Nothing, according to the poet. Actually, days in April, September, and November are equally rare, while days in February are rarer still.

Q. How do I love thee? Let me count the ways.
A. Eight.

Poetic Meter

Poetry is characterized by its use of **meter;** so to fully appreciate poetry, an understanding of poetic metrics is necessary. Besides, we will soon have to convert to the metric system.

The subject is sometimes called **prosody,** even though it deals with poetry. The primary unit of meter is called a **foot** and is composed of long and short syllables — which are not, however, called "toes." Kinds of feet are:

yam	◡ —
trophee	— ◡
spongee	— —
pterodactyl	— ◡◡
sos	··· — — — ···

A given meter is described by the kind and number of feet in a line. Three feet make a yard. Two yams make a dippity-doo.

Common English meters are the cubic diameter, the acrylic pentathlon, and the archaic tetrachloride epileptic.

Best-known is the **Heroic meter**, diagrammed thus:

— ◡◡ | ◡´Λ̈ | ✗✗ ‖ ＞＜ | ··· ‖ + ◡ ✻

and composed of a spondulix, a dipstick, two tropics separated by a diarrhea, a deckle, a caesarian, a half-gainer, and a left to the jaw.

48

English Literature

The history of literature in England begins with the anonymous epic *Beowulf*. *Beowulf*'s violent action, colorful heroes, and bizarre creatures made it popular for centuries, until it was replaced by pro wrestling.

Though the poem was composed in the eighth century, our manuscript of it contains obvious interpolations from a later period. This passage, recounting the hero's battle with the monster Godsylla, is typical.

Meanehwæl, baccat meaddehæle,   monstær lurccen;
Fulle few too many drincce,   hie luccen for fyht.
Ðen Hreorfneorhtðhwr,   son of Hrwærowþheororthwl,
Æsccen æwful jeork   to steop outsyd.
Þhud! Bashe! Crasch! Beoom!   Ðe bigge gye
Eallum his bon brak,   byt his nose offe;
Wicced Godsylla   wæld on his asse.
Monstær moppe fleor wyþ   eallum men in hælle.
Beowulf in bacceroome   fonecall bemaccen wæs;
Hearen sond of ruccus   sæd, "Hwæt ðe helle?"
Graben sheold strang   ond swich-blæd scharp
Stond feorth to fyht   ðe grimlic foe.
"Me," Godsylla sæd,   "mac ðe minsemete."
Heoro cwyc geten heold   wiþ fæmed half-nelson
Ond flyng him lic frisbe   bac to fen.
Beowulf belly up   to meaddehæle bar,
Sæd, "Ne foe beaten   mie færsom cung-fu."
Eorderen cocca-colha   yce-coeld, ðe reol þyng.

The works of Geoffrey Chaucer mark an advance in English literature, because you can almost understand them. *The Canterbury Tales* recounts the adventures of a group of pilgrims on their way to Canterbury to celebrate the first Thanksgiving with the Indians. Everyone is familiar with its lovely opening verses:

Whan Aprille shoures may coom your waie
They bringen floures that blume in Maie.
Soe if ittes rayninge have ne regrettes
Becausse itte isne rayninge rayne, I wis,
Ittes rayninge violettes.
And whan ye se clowdes uppon ye hille,
Ye soone will se crowdes of daffodilles.
Soe keepe on looken for ye bluebirde
And listning for his songe
Whan ever Aprille shoures coom alonge.

The Wife of Bath

Shakespeare

William Shakespeare — also written "Shakspere," "Shaksper," "Shaxper," "Bacon," and "Stephen King" — was the son of a simple hod-gatherer. Yet he created the greatest body of literature ever written by a man who couldn't spell his own name. His familiar phrases infest our everyday language, as can be seen from this handful of examples:

This is too much. — HENRY VIII, V.iii.85
Not so hot. — MEASURE FOR MEASURE, V.i.313
Swell. — TIMON OF ATHENS, III.v.102
Heavy. — TROILUS AND CRESSIDA, IV.v.95
Gross. — ALL'S WELL THAT ENDS WELL, I.iii.167
It is the pasture lards the rother's sides. — TIMON OF ATHENS, IV. iii.12[1]

---

1. Line numbers refer to the edition in the author's possession, with the pink cover.

title page of the octavo edition

The Octavo Edition

The literary world was stunned recently by the discovery of a lost "octavo" edition of the Bard's complete works—including several works that were previously unknown.

The various editions of Shakespeare's work are named after their discoverers—Sir Oswald Quarto, Ferenc Folio, and now Dr. Emilio Octavo, who mistakenly received the precious volume in the mail as a Book-of-the-Month Club alternate selection.

Present in the newly discovered volume are two comedies, *Something for Nothing, or, Can You Dig It?* and *All You Can Eat, or, What's It to You?*, the tragedy *Toyota and Cressida*, and a ribald poem, *The Passionate Stewardesses*. *As You Like It* appears in the octavo under its original title, *Like You Like It* — apparently changed by later emendators.

Exhaustive computer analysis of the language in the new works seems to confirm their authenticity. Only two words occur in them not used elsewhere by Shakespeare — "thermonuclear" and "jazzercise."

This passage from *Toyota and Cressida* demonstrates Shakespeare's characteristic ability to coin telling phrases, many of which are familiar despite the play's long obscurity. Typo, Duke of Earl, his army defeated by the Magnesians, is left alone on the battlefield with only his faithful retainer, Fellatio. With his plans in ruins, he falls on his dagger.

FELLATIO
Please you, my lord, lie here, 'pon this ant heap.
I'll get thee help.

TYPO
    Nay, nay, good servant; stay.
The check is in the mail, Fellatio,
Nor all our wit can call it back. 'Tis said
That toys are us, for th' gods to play withal;
Now I do think it so. Avaunt! what's here?
                    [Starts

Methinks I see mine enemy appear
With awful visage, like a rolling stone.
Then here's my sword—. Come, fiend, and make my day!
FELLATIO
[Aside] His wits are sore affected by his wound,
As one whose belt unmeetly goeth not
Through all its proper loops. I'll humour him—.
Art thou in pain from thy most grievous poke?
TYPO
Nay, only when I laugh.
                    [Dies

FELLATIO
    Thy soul is fled;
So two weeks' unpaid salary of mine
Is fled as well—and that's the bottom line.
          [He is eaten by a bear

Something for Nothing introduces one of Shakespeare's greatest clowns, Velcro. Here is a sample of his wit in an hilariously funny exchange with Flyspray, a rural constable, and Prosciutto, a fantastical Magnesian nobleman.

PROSCIUTTO
I' faith, an I had a groat I'd give thee a bull's-firkin i' the coster, to cozen thy pate withal!
VELCRO
Marry, that were a foot-monger to cry "fig" of a pox-wort.
FLYSPRAY
O thou base cutlet! thou orson welles!
VELCRO
Nay, but what a pied fitchew this fellow is! An 'twere meet, I had liefer scotch a codpiece than moble this patchy kirtle o' wits.
PROSCIUTTO
Then go to, I say! Ay, sirrah, go up and go out! Go down, go off, go home!
VELCRO
La, la, la!

FLYSPRAY
Out upon 't! Ha' mercy, i' faith! Prithee, marry! Fie! Withy phiz! Gizzle! Flmp!
          [They are eaten by a bear

Despite the passage of nearly four centuries, Shakespeare's poetry speaks to us as clearly as it did to his contemporaries. Changes in the language and the vagaries of the texts are no obstacle to understanding the universal message of Hamlet's soliloquy:

To be or not to be: that is the question:[1]
Whether 'tis nobler in the mind to suffer
The slings and arrows[2] of outrageous fortune,
Or to take arms[3] against a sea of troubles,
And by opposing end them. To die: to sleep;
No more; and by a sleep to say we end
The heartache,[4] and the thousand natural shocks
That flesh is heir to, 'tis a consummation[5]
Devoutly to be wished. To die, to sleep;
To sleep: perchance to dream: ay, there's the rub;[6]
For in that sleep of death what dreams may come,
When we have shuffled off this mortal coil,[7]
Must give us pause: there's the respect
That makes calamity of so long life;[8]
For who would bear the whips and scorns[9] of time,
The oppressor's wrong, the proud man's contumely,*
The pangs of despised[10] love,[11] the law's delay,
The insolence of office, and the spurns
That patient merit of the unworthy takes,[12]
When he himself might his quietus** make
With a bare bodkin?† Who would fardels‡ bear
To grunt and sweat under a weary life,
But that the dread of something after death,[13]
The undiscovered country from whose bourn§
No traveler returns,[14] puzzles the will,
Creeps in this petty pace from day to day,
And makes us rather bear those ills[15] we have
Than fly to others we know not of?
Thus conscience does make cowards[16] of us all,
And thus the native hue of resolution[17]
Is sicklied o'er with the pale cast of thought,
And enterprises of great pitch and moment[18]
With this regard their currents turn awry
And lose the name of action. —Soft you now![19]
—HAMLET, PRINCE OF DENMARK,[20] ACT III, SC. i

1. Flumson suggests, "To be or not to be that. Is the question / Whether 'tis nobler . . ." which provides the missing verb for the second sentence. Freebish conjectures, "To be or not to be. —what was the question?" which effectively depicts Hamlet's confused state of mind but requires the period followed by the dash—rare in Shakespeare's plays of this period.

2. The quarto gives "stings and arrows." Ferguson suggests, "bows and arrows." The octavo has "chutes and ladders."

3. The octavo reads "take Dramamine," which is nicely consistent with the metaphor.

4. Folio: "headache." Octavo: "stomachache."

5. The octavo gives "consommé."

6. Flower's emendation: "ay, there's the trouble." Octavo: "Hey, where's my socks?"

7. The quarto reads, "shoveled off this mortal soil"; Smyth suggests, "sputtered off this mortal oil." The octavo has "shuffled off to Buffalo."

8. Sithers's ingenious emendation is: "That makes calamity of 'So long, Life!'"

9. Ferguson suggests, "whips and chains"; Sithers suggests, "whips and ropes"; Smyth suggests whips and rubber underwear at his place.

10. The quarto has "disprized," which Flumson emends to "displaced," and Smyth to "distrest." The octavo has "decaffeinated."

11. Perhaps a veiled reference to the mysterious "Avon lady" of the sonnets.

12. Possibly an allusion to either Edward I or Heinrich of Magnesia.

13. Flumson reads, "the dead of something after earth"; Freebish's emendation is: "the bread of something after dearth."

14. This image was picked up and reused in a poem by Edna St. Vincent de Paul.

15. Ferguson: "bare those quills." Octavo: "wrestle those bears."

16. The octavo's "custards" is clearly erroneous.

17. Cf. Spenser's *Dairy Queen*.

18. Folio: "pith and moment." Octavo: "pith and vinegar."

19. Octavo: ". . . of action, don't you know."

20. The title is given in the first folio as *The Tragedy of Hamlet, Prince of Denmark*. It is undoubtedly the same play that appears as *The Tragedie of Amlette* in the Stationer's Register for 1602. The octavo gives it as *Omelette, Hash Browns, and a Danish*.

*Contumely: a rough, hooded garment; also, a disease of sheep

**Quietus: a kind of porridge made with groats; also, a disease of sheep

†Bodkin: a small cooking vessel much like the modern frimmager—here used as a punning sexual reference; also, a sexual disease of sheep

‡Fardels: same as furdels; also, a disease of sheep

§Bourn: a minor rural official—hence by extension any public convenience, such as a restroom; also, a disease of sheep

The Novel

The English novel was pioneered in the eighteenth century by writers such as Richardson, Sterne, and Defoe (who wrote the harrowing *Journal of the Pledge Night*). The form was at first decried as vulgar, immoral, and dangerous by social critics. As a result it was very successful.

In later centuries, the novel was recognized as the crown of literary endeavor, and became a part of every school curriculum. As a result the typical serious novel is now read by five hundred people at the

outside, all of whom write for the *New York Review of Books*.

The form, however, remains a rewarding one, provided the author can sell the movie rights.

LEADING NOVELS RATED

When shopping for novels, let the buyer beware! Many of the models we tested were poorly constructed, excessively slow, or hard to start. Patronize only reputable dealers and be sure to ask about the guarantee. A colorful, attractive cover is usually a sign of a sturdy novel; look especially for embossing, foil stamping, and die-cutting.

AUTHOR	TITLE	EXCITING PARTS	DIRTY PARTS	FUNNY STUFF	TOO LONG	MOVIE VERSIONS	TOTAL
Austen, Jane	Pride and Prejudice					✓	1
Brontë, Emily	Wuthering Heights					✓	1
Cervantes, Miguel de	Don Quixote	✓			✓	✓	1
Conrad, Joseph	Lord Jim	✓				✓	2
Cooper, James Fenimore	The Deerslayer	✓✓				✓	3
Dickens, Charles	A Tale of Two Cities	✓✓				✓	3
Dos Passos, John	U.S.A.				✓✓		−2
Dostoevsky, Feodor	Crime and Punishment				✓✓	✓	−1
Dreiser, Theodore	An American Tragedy				✓	✓	0
Dumas, Alexandre	The Three Musketeers	✓✓				✓✓✓	5
Eliot, George	The Mill on the Floss						0
Flaubert, Gustave	Madame Bovary					✓	1
Hardy, Thomas	The Return of the Native						0
Hawthorne, Nathaniel	The Scarlet Letter					✓	1
Hugo, Victor	Les Misérables	✓				✓	2
James, Henry	The Turn of the Screw					✓	1
Joyce, James	Ulysses		✓		✓✓	✓	0
Lawrence, D. H.	Lady Chatterley's Lover		✓✓			✓	3
Mann, Thomas	The Magic Mountain						0
Melville, Herman	Moby Dick	✓✓			✓✓	✓✓	2
Proust, Marcel	Remembrance of Things Past				✓✓✓		−3
Scott, Sir Walter	Ivanhoe	✓✓				✓✓✓	5
Steinbeck, John	Of Mice and Men	✓				✓	2
Stendhal	The Red and the Black				✓✓		−2
Swift, Jonathan	Gulliver's Travels	✓		✓		✓✓✓	5
Thackeray, William M.	Vanity Fair					✓	1
Tolstoy, Leo	War and Peace				✓✓	✓	−1
Trollope, Anthony	Barchester Towers				✓✓		−2
Twain, Mark	Tom Sawyer	✓		✓✓		✓✓✓✓	7

SOURCE: ART CONSUMER REPORTS   too long = points off

The Decline and Fall of the Roman Empire BY EDWARD GIBBON

*Deluxe
Coffee Table
Edition*

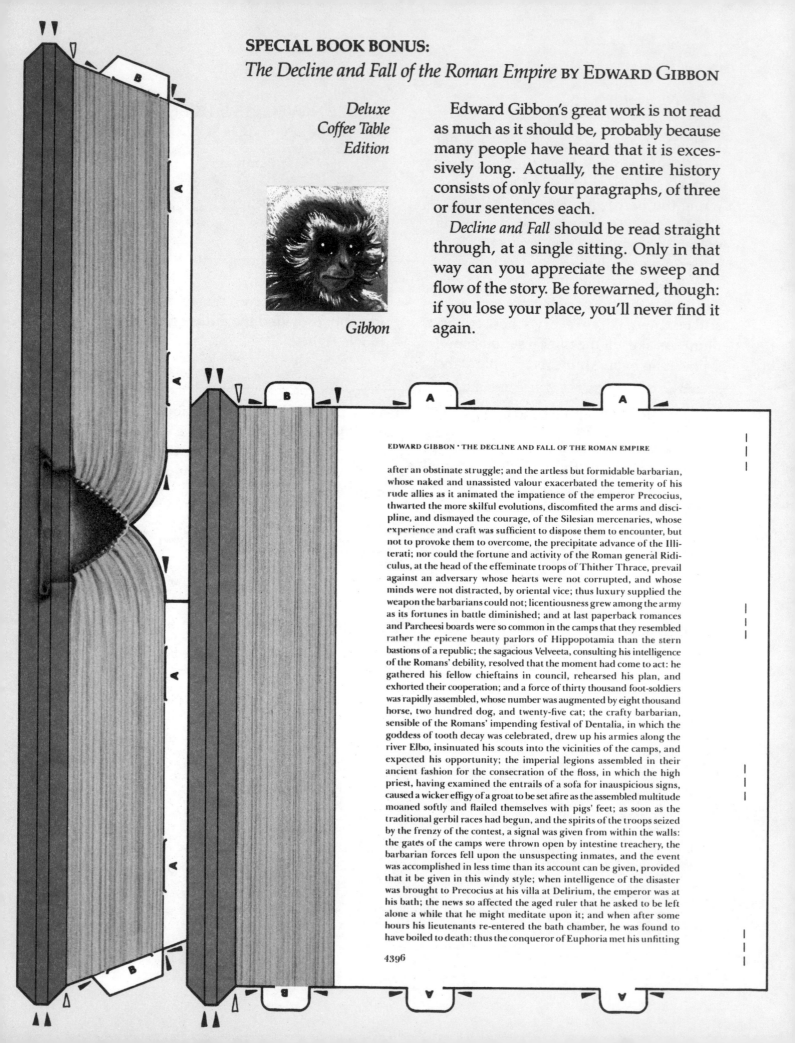

Gibbon

Edward Gibbon's great work is not read as much as it should be, probably because many people have heard that it is excessively long. Actually, the entire history consists of only four paragraphs, of three or four sentences each.

Decline and Fall should be read straight through, at a single sitting. Only in that way can you appreciate the sweep and flow of the story. Be forewarned, though: if you lose your place, you'll never find it again.

EDWARD GIBBON · THE DECLINE AND FALL OF THE ROMAN EMPIRE

after an obstinate struggle; and the artless but formidable barbarian, whose naked and unassisted valour exacerbated the temerity of his rude allies as it animated the impatience of the emperor Precocius, thwarted the more skilful evolutions, discomfited the arms and discipline, and dismayed the courage, of the Silesian mercenaries, whose experience and craft was sufficient to dispose them to encounter, but not to provoke them to overcome, the precipitate advance of the Illiterati; nor could the fortune and activity of the Roman general Ridiculus, at the head of the effeminate troops of Thither Thrace, prevail against an adversary whose hearts were not corrupted, and whose minds were not distracted, by oriental vice; thus luxury supplied the weapon the barbarians could not; licentiousness grew among the army as its fortunes in battle diminished; and at last paperback romances and Parcheesi boards were so common in the camps that they resembled rather the epicene beauty parlors of Hippopotamia than the stern bastions of a republic; the sagacious Velveeta, consulting his intelligence of the Romans' debility, resolved that the moment had come to act: he gathered his fellow chieftains in council, rehearsed his plan, and exhorted their cooperation; and a force of thirty thousand foot-soldiers was rapidly assembled, whose number was augmented by eight thousand horse, two hundred dog, and twenty-five cat; the crafty barbarian, sensible of the Romans' impending festival of Dentalia, in which the goddess of tooth decay was celebrated, drew up his armies along the river Elbo, insinuated his scouts into the vicinities of the camps, and expected his opportunity; the imperial legions assembled in their ancient fashion for the consecration of the floss, in which the high priest, having examined the entrails of a sofa for inauspicious signs, caused a wicker effigy of a groat to be set afire as the assembled multitude moaned softly and flailed themselves with pigs' feet; as soon as the traditional gerbil races had begun, and the spirits of the troops seized by the frenzy of the contest, a signal was given from within the walls: the gates of the camps were thrown open by intestine treachery, the barbarian forces fell upon the unsuspecting inmates, and the event was accomplished in less time than its account can be given, provided that it be given in this windy style; when intelligence of the disaster was brought to Precocius at his villa at Delirium, the emperor was at his bath; the news so affected the aged ruler that he asked to be left alone a while that he might meditate upon it; and when after some hours his lieutenants re-entered the bath chamber, he was found to have boiled to death: thus the conqueror of Euphoria met his unfitting

4396

1. Cut out all parts along the heavy black lines. Fold UP along lines marked by open arrows. Fold DOWN along lines marked by solid arrows.

2. Staple left and right pages together at the dashed lines.

3. Insert tabs A into slots A. Insert tabs B into slots B on all four corners.

4. Cut a 6⅜" × 9¾" piece of corrugated cardboard. Glue flaps of book around all four edges of cardboard.

▷ = fold up
▶ = fold down
- - - = staple

9¾"
6⅜"

glue

Position finished book on coffee table so as to cover cigarette burn. You can be confident no one will ever pick it up.

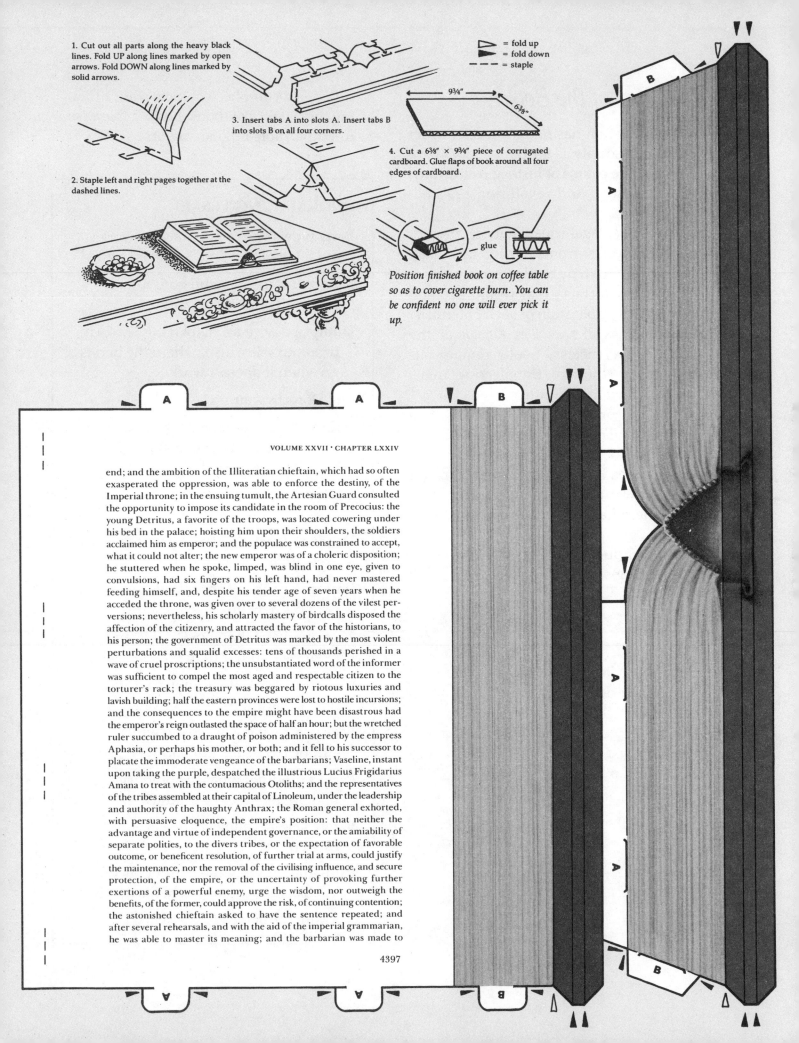

A   A   B

VOLUME XXVII · CHAPTER LXXIV

end; and the ambition of the Illiteratian chieftain, which had so often exasperated the oppression, was able to enforce the destiny, of the Imperial throne; in the ensuing tumult, the Artesian Guard consulted the opportunity to impose its candidate in the room of Precocius: the young Detritus, a favorite of the troops, was located cowering under his bed in the palace; hoisting him upon their shoulders, the soldiers acclaimed him as emperor; and the populace was constrained to accept, what it could not alter; the new emperor was of a choleric disposition; he stuttered when he spoke, limped, was blind in one eye, given to convulsions, had six fingers on his left hand, had never mastered feeding himself, and, despite his tender age of seven years when he acceded the throne, was given over to several dozens of the vilest perversions; nevertheless, his scholarly mastery of birdcalls disposed the affection of the citizenry, and attracted the favor of the historians, to his person; the government of Detritus was marked by the most violent perturbations and squalid excesses: tens of thousands perished in a wave of cruel proscriptions; the unsubstantiated word of the informer was sufficient to compel the most aged and respectable citizen to the torturer's rack; the treasury was beggared by riotous luxuries and lavish building; half the eastern provinces were lost to hostile incursions; and the consequences to the empire might have been disastrous had the emperor's reign outlasted the space of half an hour; but the wretched ruler succumbed to a draught of poison administered by the empress Aphasia, or perhaps his mother, or both; and it fell to his successor to placate the immoderate vengeance of the barbarians; Vaseline, instant upon taking the purple, despatched the illustrious Lucius Frigidarius Amana to treat with the contumacious Otoliths; and the representatives of the tribes assembled at their capital of Linoleum, under the leadership and authority of the haughty Anthrax; the Roman general exhorted, with persuasive eloquence, the empire's position: that neither the advantage and virtue of independent governance, or the amiability of separate polities, to the divers tribes, or the expectation of favorable outcome, or beneficent resolution, of further trial at arms, could justify the maintenance, nor the removal of the civilising influence, and secure protection, of the empire, or the uncertainty of provoking further exertions of a powerful enemy, urge the wisdom, nor outweigh the benefits, of the former, could approve the risk, of continuing contention; the astonished chieftain asked to have the sentence repeated; and after several rehearsals, and with the aid of the imperial grammarian, he was able to master its meaning; and the barbarian was made to

4397

A   A   B

The Art of the Book

No invention has had as much impact on human society as the book. Books have changed the course of history, overthrown great empires, and revolutionized individual lives.

Of course, legal considerations prevent modern books from risking any such results. (Most publishers now carry insurance contracts that would prohibit the original publication of such potentially actionable works as *Das Kapital* or the Bible.) Nevertheless, books remain our primary method of transferring information, next to computers.

The first printed book was the Gutenberg Bible. There was no system for distributing books yet, so Gutenberg had to leave copies in motel rooms. As a result he soon went bankrupt, a tradition that publishers have regularly observed ever since.

The production of the modern book, or "reading support system" as it is now called, is a complex technical craft, utilizing the services of thousands of otherwise unemployable English majors.

THE DEWEY DECIMAL SYSTEM

Thomas E. Dewey was born in 1902 in Owosso, Michigan. However, he had nothing to do with the book cataloging system, which was invented by a different Dewey. The original system has recently been revised to better reflect the nature of modern publishing:

000–299 cookbooks
300–499 diet books
500–599 computer books
600–699 how-to books
700–799 humor books
800–899 pop-up books
900–999 other

BOOKMAKING TERMS

Body type: type of person who works out a lot; also called "superior figure"

Dummy: someone who goes into publishing for the money

Dump: a device for displaying books to promote sales; also, where the books go when it doesn't work

Em: Dorothy's aunt

Galley: type of ship, where authors often work part-time to supplement their income

Gutter: source of material for humor books

Headband: article worn by editors who grew up in the '60s

Imposition: an author asking a friend to read his new ms.

Mass market: what movies, TV, and businesses other than books have

Ms., mss.: books by unmarried and married authors, respectively

Page proofs: copy of ms. on which author writes his final draft

Perfect binding: what the bindery seldom manages to produce

Ragged right: followers of Reverend Falwell

Run-around: what the editor gets when he asks the author where his ms. is

Stick-up capital: New York City

A Typical Book Page

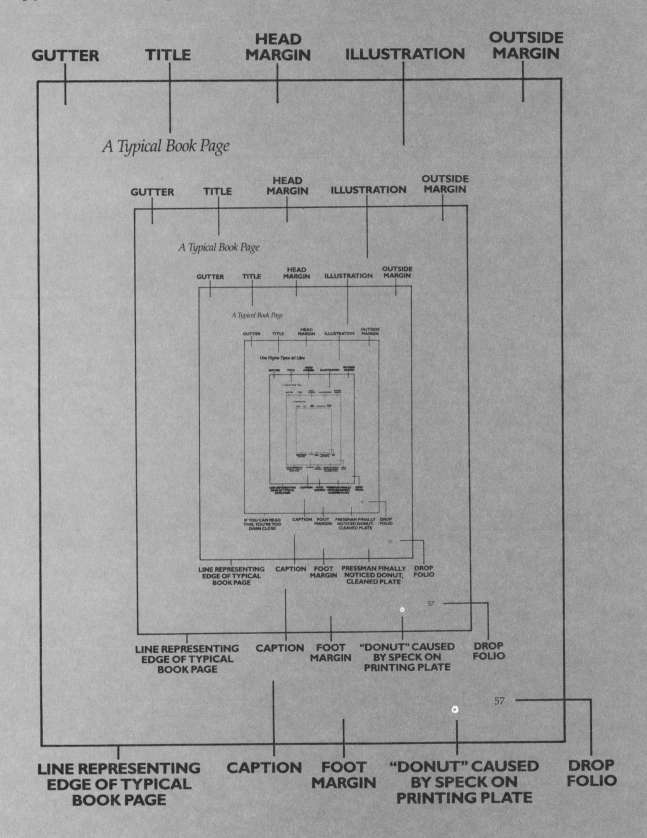

GUTTER **TITLE** **HEAD MARGIN** **ILLUSTRATION** **OUTSIDE MARGIN**

A Typical Book Page

LINE REPRESENTING EDGE OF TYPICAL BOOK PAGE **CAPTION** **FOOT MARGIN** **"DONUT" CAUSED BY SPECK ON PRINTING PLATE** **DROP FOLIO**

Understanding Book Codes

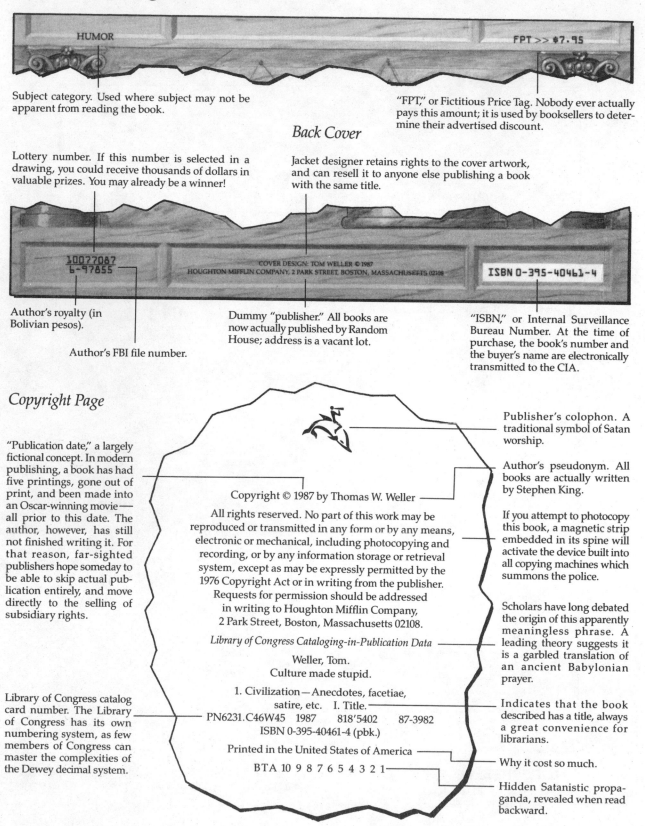

HUMOR

FPT >> $7.95

Subject category. Used where subject may not be apparent from reading the book.

"FPT," or Fictitious Price Tag. Nobody ever actually pays this amount; it is used by booksellers to determine their advertised discount.

Back Cover

Lottery number. If this number is selected in a drawing, you could receive thousands of dollars in valuable prizes. You may already be a winner!

Jacket designer retains rights to the cover artwork, and can resell it to anyone else publishing a book with the same title.

10077087
6-97855

COVER DESIGN: TOM WELLER © 1987
HOUGHTON MIFFLIN COMPANY, 2 PARK STREET, BOSTON, MASSACHUSETTS 02108

ISBN 0-395-40461-4

Author's royalty (in Bolivian pesos).

Author's FBI file number.

Dummy "publisher." All books are now actually published by Random House; address is a vacant lot.

"ISBN," or Internal Surveillance Bureau Number. At the time of purchase, the book's number and the buyer's name are electronically transmitted to the CIA.

Copyright Page

"Publication date," a largely fictional concept. In modern publishing, a book has had five printings, gone out of print, and been made into an Oscar-winning movie— all prior to this date. The author, however, has still not finished writing it. For that reason, far-sighted publishers hope someday to be able to skip actual publication entirely, and move directly to the selling of subsidiary rights.

Publisher's colophon. A traditional symbol of Satan worship.

Author's pseudonym. All books are actually written by Stephen King.

If you attempt to photocopy this book, a magnetic strip embedded in its spine will activate the device built into all copying machines which summons the police.

Library of Congress Cataloging-in-Publication Data

Weller, Tom.
Culture made stupid.

1. Civilization—Anecdotes, facetiae, satire, etc.   I. Title.
PN6231.C46W45   1987   818'5402   87-3982
ISBN 0-395-40461-4 (pbk.)

Printed in the United States of America

BTA 10 9 8 7 6 5 4 3 2 1

Scholars have long debated the origin of this apparently meaningless phrase. A leading theory suggests it is a garbled translation of an ancient Babylonian prayer.

Indicates that the book described has a title, always a great convenience for librarians.

Why it cost so much.

Hidden Satanistic propaganda, revealed when read backward.

Library of Congress catalog card number. The Library of Congress has its own numbering system, as few members of Congress can master the complexities of the Dewey decimal system.

V. The Useful Arts

Faith without works is a lot easier.
  —St. Paul, Minnesota

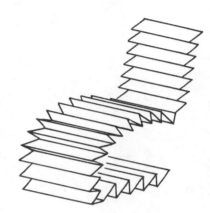

Mies van der Ow
"Buzz saw" chair, 1925
With this design, van der Ow redefined the
traditional concept of a chair as a place to sit.

THE DISTINCTION between fine art and mere utilitarian craft seems clear-cut. No useful, productive, or necessary work can truly share the prestige of art. A person who makes a work of art—say, by spending a few hours crumpling up old newspapers and throwing them on the floor of a museum—is an *artist*; he will be interviewed, written about in books, given awards, invited to parties. A person who produces something useful—say, by working hard and faithfully for thirty years manufacturing basic foodstuffs or bricks—is of no interest.

Generally, if it's good for anything, it's not art.

Yet there is a middle ground. Some of the so-called applied arts can aspire to uselessness; and to the extent that they do, they can share some of the reflected glory of art. An architect whose building does not keep out the rain; a filmmaker who makes a dull, incomprehensible movie; a graphic designer who renders a book unreadable: these rise above the level of ordinary craft and become worthy of serious attention.

60

Architecture

Egypt

Among the oldest works of architecture are the pyramids of Egypt. They were provided with every amenity, so that the Pharaohs who were entombed there could enjoy themselves in the afterworld as they had in life. Chief among these luxuries, of course, was sharp razor blades.

cross section, pyramid of Pharaoh Osmosis

air channels

king's chamber

master bath

sauna

corridor

redwood deck

entrance

guest chamber

laundry/ utility

kitchenette / breakfast nook

screening room

rumpus room / bar

bowling alley

garage

CAPITALS

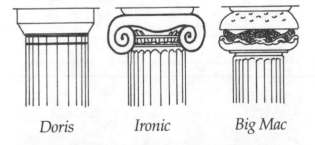

Doris   *Ironic*   *Big Mac*

the classical institution of capital punishment

Greece and Rome

The Greeks developed one of the world's great architectural styles. There were various **orders** of building, each typified by its columns. The three main styles of column were **Doris, Ironic,** and **Gossip.**

Another type, the **Composite,** was sometimes used when the architect had to deal with both the client and the client's wife. The rumored existence of a fifth column is unverified.

ORNAMENTS

egg-and-dart

egg-and-bacon

PARTS OF A CLASSICAL TEMPLE

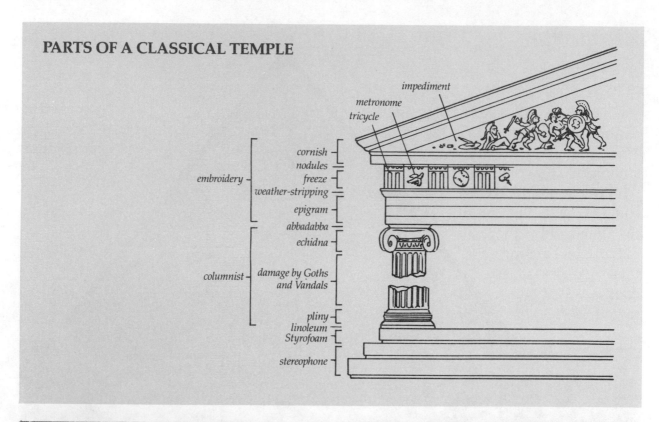

- impediment
- metronome
- tricycle

embroidery
- cornish
- nodules
- freeze
- weather-stripping
- epigram

columnist
- abbadabba
- echidna
- damage by Goths and Vandals
- pliny
- linoleum
- Styrofoam
- stereophone

Reconstructed view of the interior of the Baths of Caracalla

The Romans applied Greek concepts of architecture to a wide range of practical structures — roads, aqueducts, bus stations, and public buildings such as the magnificent Baths of Caracalla.

The Middle Ages

When bathing went out of fashion in the Middle Ages, there was no need for elaborate public baths. Medieval people devoted the spare time thus freed to the construction of Gothic cathedrals.

The invention of the **vault** made this style of building possible. Prior to the vault, the money for large constructions would invariably disappear before the project was finished.

Cathedral of St. Pancreas

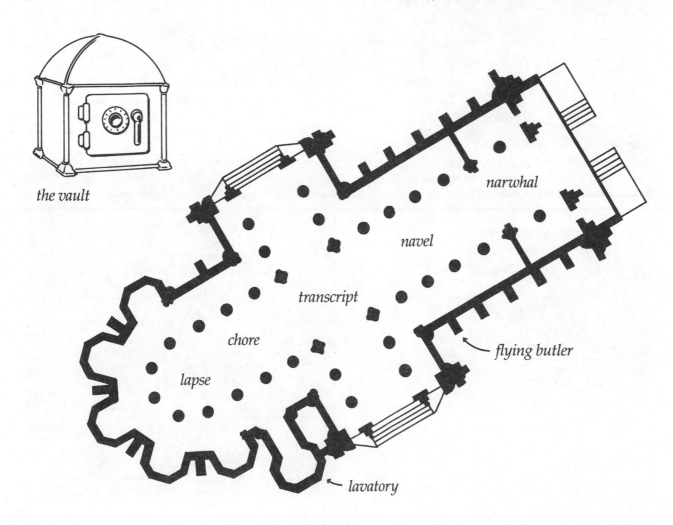

the vault

narwhal

navel

transcript

chore

lapse

← *flying butler*

← *lavatory*

Frank Lloyd Wrong: An American Original

Frank Lloyd Wrong (1869–1959) was the most daring innovator in modern American architecture. His works still stand — at least those that haven't fallen down — as the best exemplars of his famous dicta: "Form follows the down payment" and "Less is cheaper."

Wrong's first major work was the Hall of Cellophane at the 1893 Yuba City World's Fair. This structure marked the first use of prestressed linoleum trusses, as well as the last.

The famous Flatiron Building in Eerie, Pennsylvania, was the first skyscraper (since demolished to make way for a steam-and-dry model).

The "Prairie House" was Wrong's attempt to harmonize the building with the landscape.

A typical detail of a Wrong interior.

"Falling House" was a further step in integrating the structure with its surroundings. Its final form was made possible by the use of cantilevered concrete slabs from the low-bidding contractor.

Current Trends in Architecture

Many contemporary architects find the dominant "international style" cold, faceless, and oppressive. A style called **post-modern** has arisen in reaction to it. Post-modernism is characterized by a return to ornamentation, often employing traditional forms. To better understand this revolutionary, up-to-the-minute trend, review the section on classical orders of columns (page 61).

hotel lobby, Miasma, Florida

spare, impersonal international style   *post-modern reform*

post-modern approach to a private home

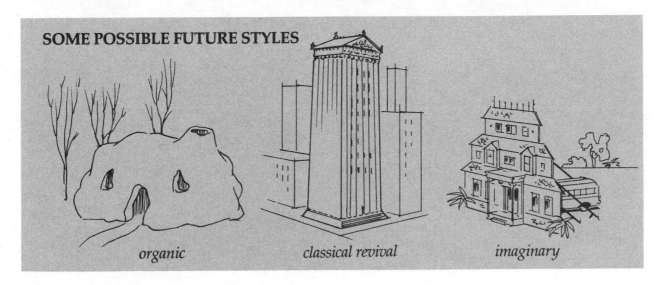

SOME POSSIBLE FUTURE STYLES

organic   *classical revival*   *imaginary*

The Cinema

Jean-Luc Godard defined film as "the truth, twenty-four times a second."[1] Others have called it "stunning . . . a masterwork" (Vincent Canby, *New York Times*); "a must-see" (Richard Corliss, *Time*); "if you see only one twentieth-century art form this year, this should be it" (Judith H. Crist, WOR-TV); "a lot of fun . . . take the kids" (Roger Ebert, *Chicago Sun-Times*); and "★ ★ ★ ½" (*New York Daily News*).

The history of the film begins in ancient Rome. The first film ever made was *Quo Vadis* in AD 12. It was very popular; one reviewer said, "If you see only one film this year, it has to be *Quo Vadis*." Later Roman films developed into elaborate productions, many boasting casts of Ms.

The Roman heritage persists: even today, film titles often use Roman numerals.

The cinema fell into decline in medieval times. Projectors turned by yoked oxen and parchment film—the sprocket holes painstakingly hand-cut by monks—made for a cumbersome system. Films such as *Roland Meets the Green Knight* are difficult for the modern viewer on account of the absence of perspective in the photography and the incorrect anatomy of the actors.

The perfection of the film has been attributed variously to Edison, Friese-Greene, or the Lumières. Probably the real credit for the success of the cinema belongs to Bucyrus Entwhistle, who invented the Junior Mint. Film historians have been unable, however, to unearth any information about a Senior Mint.

---

1. "I Auteur Be in Pictures," *Cashiers du Cinema*, no. 31, January 1954.

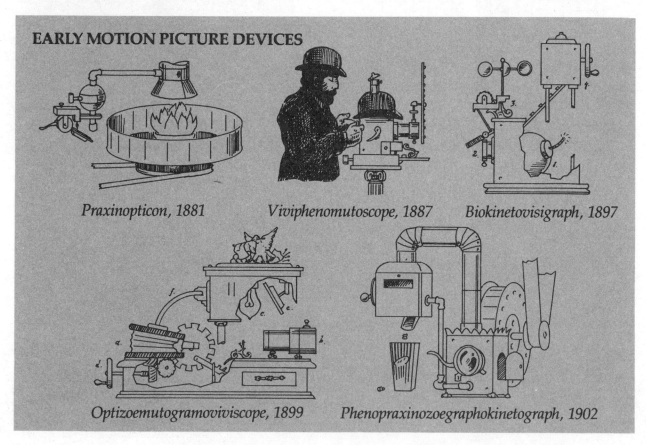

EARLY MOTION PICTURE DEVICES

Praxinopticon, 1881   *Viviphenomutoscope, 1887*   *Biokinetovisigraph, 1897*

Optizoemutogramoviviscope, 1899   *Phenopraxinozoegraphokinetograph, 1902*

The Problem of Film Preservation

Today, after years of neglect, there is a growing awareness of the problem of film preservation. Thousands, if not tens of thousands, of films have vanished utterly, through carelessness or decay.

Although much has been done, much remains to be done. Thousands of films survive, in attics and dusty archives, ready to be revived unless action is taken. Thousands more circulate in large numbers, passed off as "classics."

Anyone who has experienced von Stroheim's *Greed* can imagine the unbearable agony of sitting through the original version, before wise studio executives shortened it by two-thirds. Yet many similar films exist in their full, excessive lengths.

The American Film Preservation Insti-

Famous early film that settled an age-old debate: is there a point at which all four hooves of a galloping horse are off the ground? To everyone's surprise, it was proved that at no time during a gallop does any *hoof touch the ground.*

tute has a program to track down and destroy rumored prints of such films. At its laboratory in Lake Turgid, New York, old film can be safely incinerated. The director, Flinders R. Paddock, remarks, "It's the innocent that suffer most. Some unscrupulous film society advertises something as 'the greatest film of all time,' and college students will come see it — what do they know? — and it's this damn thing in black and white, silent, made in Russia or someplace, and goes on for *hours.*"

He shudders at the thought.

"When it happens to kids, sometimes they never get over it. I think it was seeing *The Loon's Necklace* four times in school that got me started in this work."

Documentaries, of course, are a large part of the Institute's work. "Also any animated films that don't have Bugs Bunny or Donald Duck or something good. *Fiddle-Dee-Dee*, there's one on our list," says Paddock.

"And then the old standbys — all of Pudovkin, for instance. It's a big job."

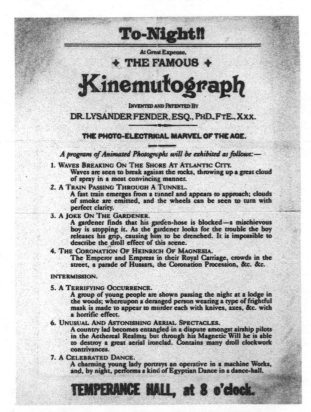

Handbill for early motion picture exhibition

Unusual Film Formats

FLOOR-O-SCOPE®
Introduced during World War II; The Enemy Below and Thirty Seconds Over Tokyo were originally released in this format.

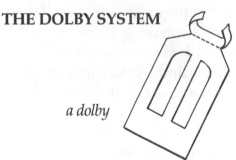

VERTISCOPE™
An extremely tall, narrow format ideal for films about mountain climbing or skyscrapers.

DIMENTIRAMA™
This short-lived 3-D process involved a bank of mechanical devices behind a flexible rubber screen.

SUPERTOTALSCOPE®
The audience was suspended inside a completely spherical screen. Though the first production, This is Supertotalscope, boasted stunning photography of a trip through a cow's intestinal tract, the process was a commercial failure.

THE DOLBY SYSTEM

a dolby

The sound quality of today's motion pictures is greatly enhanced by the use of the dolby. A dolby is that strange-shaped piece of cardboard that comes wrapped inside new shirts. It was discovered a few years ago that this device, when built into a recording system, would filter unwanted noise from the audio track. The unwanted noise could then be collected and sold to producers of heavy metal records.

INVOLVAVISION®
In this unusual process, the film was projected directly onto the audience.

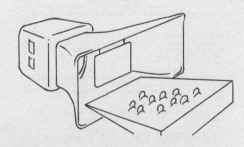

MEGALOPHONIC™ SOUND
No one was admitted without a certificate from an ear doctor.

RATINGS

The motion picture industry's rating board, in order to provide parents and other moviegoers with more information, has developed these new rating categories:

G-10	For general audiences—hero is ten years old
GD	Hero is a cocker spaniel—diabetics should exercise caution
G-15	All characters are under 15
GL	All characters are constructed of latex
G-17	Youth comedy—adults not admitted unless accompanied by person under 17
PS	For mature young people—heroine keeps sheet wrapped around her chest in bedroom scenes
PD	Parental discretion advised—character uses a gratuitous dirty word in order to avoid a G rating
RS	For mature audiences—characters take gratuitous showers throughout
RT	Chain saws, drills, and other power tools used
XG	Only licensed gynecologists admitted
F***	Star is comedian whose dialogue consists entirely of dirty words
P	Pop music score—may be unsuitable for Max Steiner fans
EL	Subtitles in extra large type for those over 40
C-60	Closing credits run for more than an hour
?	Close-captioned for the stupid
C$	Candy bar costs more than $2.50
S	Soundtrack of picture in adjacent theater clearly audible
D	Audience will be hit for charitable donation before film
HBO	You can catch this picture on the cable in about a week

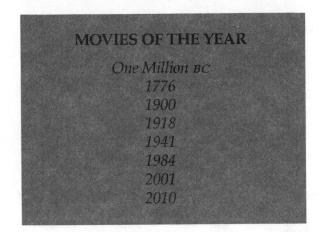

MOVIES OF THE YEAR

One Million BC
1776
1900
1918
1941
1984
2001
2010

RECOMMENDED FILMS

The serious student of the cinema can view these classic works through university extension programs or local film societies.

Attack of the Men in Rubber Suits
The Creature That Was Pulled Along on Wires
Planet of the Bad Dubbing
The Movie That Wouldn't Die
Actresses from Hell
Love Slaves of the Producer
Island of the Tax Break
It Came from the Prop Department
Battle of the Model Spaceships
I Was the Director's Girlfriend

QUIZ

In this list of film credits, explain what each person does.

1. For 10 points each:
key grip
dolly grip
best boy

2. For 20 points each:
clapper loader
Foley walker
DGA trainee

3. For 1,000,000 points:
executive producer

Graphic Design

The graphic designer's goal is to render printed material readable, attractive, and profitable to himself, not necessarily in that order. The corporate logo is a typical task; the designer must combine art and typography in a way that makes a bold, unambiguous statement about the client's product.

Logo for a management consulting firm symbolizes efficient, productive results of their services.

Distinctive graphic treatment of lettering helps make this firm name memorable.

Logo for multinational consortium with wide-ranging, expanding interests.

Stylized building suggests stability; slanted type conveys firm's willingness to experiment with creative financial techniques.

Stylized hand makes an unmistakable graphic connection with the product.

Logo for a small regional airline conveys sense of speed, geographical connection.

The designer selects typefaces on the basis of appearance, appropriateness, and by throwing darts at a chart like this. ▶

Chart of Type Styles

ACCIDENT
ABCD abcd

BASKETBALL
ABCD abcd

BAUWAU
ABCD abcd

BAUWAU UGLY
ABCD abcde

BAUWAU OPPRESSIVE
ABCD abcde

BIMBO
ABCD abc

BOLONI
ABCD abcd

BOOKIE
ABCD abc

BUCKLER WITH SWASH
ABCD abcd

BUD LIGHT
ABCD abcde

CLICHÉ
ABCD abcd

CLICHÉ SILLY
ABCD abcd

DAMSEL DISTRESSED
ABCD ab

FASCISMA
ABCD abcd

5 O'CLOCK SHADOW
ABCD

FUTURE IMPERFECT
ABCD abcdω

GAUDY
ABCD abcd

GAUDY BADSTYLE
ABCD abcd

HAPPY MEDIUM

ABCD abcde

HEAD LIGHT
ABCD

HERO BOLD
ABCD abcde

HERO BOLD WITH SWASH
ABCD abcd

INVISIBLE

MEMPHIS TENNESSEE

ABCD abcd

MICROSCOPIC
ABCD abcde

MILK CONDENSED
ABCD abcde

MISTRIAL
ABCD abcde

MOVIE SCRIPT
ABCD abcde

NYLON
ABCD abcd

NYLON SEMI-SWEET
ABCD abcd

PEIGNOIR
ABCD abcde

PEIGNOIR EXTRA UGLY
ABCD abcd

PESSIMA
ABCD abcd

PESSIMA EXCESSIVE
ABCD abcd

PICKLE
ABCD

POLIO BLACK
ABCD abc

POLIO BLACK & BLUE
ABCD abc

REPULSIVE GROTESQUE
ABCD

TIMES UP
ABCD abc

TIMES A-WASTIN'
ABCD abc

TIMES THEY ARE A-CHANGIN'
ABCD abcd

TRENDY ILLEGIBLE
ABCD abc

VELVEETICA
ABCD abcd

VELVEETICA OVERUSED
ABCD abcd

VENUSIAN
♯ ☮ © ♂

WINDOW DISPLAY
ABCD ab

ZILCH
ABCD abc

ZILCH UNREADABLE
ABCD ab

A Redesign for the United States

In commemoration of the bicentennial of the Constitution, the government commissioned the New York design firm of Trivelpiece, Afterburner, and Spoor to develop a corporate identity program for the nation. Here is a first look at America's new image.

NAME
New name for the country is shorter, punchier, and boasts a distinctive typographic treatment. The traditional star has also gotten a facelift.

...because we're people working together with people who care about people.

MOTTO
Old motto was in Latin. New motto communicates the goals of the country in modern terms.

FLAG
Old design was cluttered. New design reduces stars to one, while the stripe motif is subtly echoed by diagonal pinstripes. Old red, white, and blue colors will be shifted slightly toward a more sophisticated scheme of terra cotta, crème, and teal.

STAMPS
Product code will eliminate the need to print new stamps when rates change.

THE PRESIDENTIAL SEAL

CURRENCY
Livelier design will be printed on recycled, biodegradable paper.

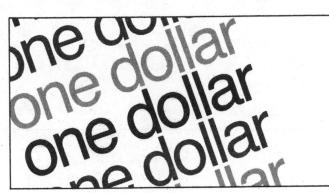

UniSAM

UniSARM
UniSEA
UniSAIR

ARMED FORCES
Stylish uniforms will complement the new names of the services.

SYMBOL
Stern, aged "Uncle Sam" presented a negative image. The designers collaborated with Marvel Comics to design a younger, more vigorous character, now called simply "Sam."

FORMS OF ADDRESS

President of the U.S.: Sir, My dear Mr. President, You damned fool

Vice President of the U.S.: Whatsisname

Speaker of the House: Your Verbosity

Senator: Your Platitude

Representative: Your Ineptitude

Judge: Your Hardship

Captain of a ship: Your Latitude

Admiral: Your Battleship

Registrar: Your Registry

Basketball player: Your Altitude

Dame: Madam

Madam: Dame

Duke: Your Disgrace

Earl: Your Earliness

Viscount: Your Viscosity

Duke of Earl: Oh wo-wo-o yi-yi-yi-i-i

Marquis: What's playing?

Abbot: Hey, Abbot!

Abbey: Dear Abbey

Master of the Rolls: Pass the rolls

Privy Councillor: Excuse me, where's the restroom?

PROOOFREADERS' MARKS

⌒	Close up
⌒→	Close up and go home
♪	Take out
↦	Eat here
∧	Campgrounds, next exit
⊏	Move to left
⊐	Move to right
⊓	Stand up
⊔	Sit down
⍾	Fight, fight, fight
wf	Insert barking dog
✗	Bad letter
✗✗	Very bad letter
✗✗✗	Send letter to bed without supper
bf	Boldfaced lie

cap	Take off your cap
stet	Take off your Stetson
s.c.	South Carolina
SP	Southern Pacific
✎	Editor sharpening pencil
?	Query author
#@*?!	Tell author what you think of him
#	Challenge author to tick-tack-toe by mail
//	Straighten out author
↓	Push down letter
↖	Push author off cliff
tr	Throw ms. in trash
℈	Delete reference to vegetable

A PLACE-SETTING FOR A SIMPLE DINNER

A well-set table adds much to the enjoyment of a meal. One does well to master the few simple rules that govern correct use of each implement—since the slightest error in usage will utterly ruin an otherwise elegant dinner, and bring irreparable social disgrace on the perpetrator. Just remember to begin at the outside and work to the inside, from the right or the left alternating with the courses, except for clear soups, desserts, and Thursdays, and in months with no "r," when the order is reversed.

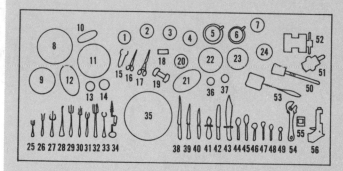

1. Sauterne glass
2. Rhine wine glass
3. Claret glass
4. Brandy snifter
5. Tea cup
6. Demitasse
7. Water glass
8. Salad plate
9. Bread plate
10. Butter plate
11. Cold soup bowl
12. Hot soup bowl
13. Finger bowl
14. Thumb bowl
15. Crouton tongs
16. Grape scissors
17. Mozzarella scissors
18. Napkin ring
19. Knife rest
20. Oil cruet
21. Asparagus plate
22. Artichoke plate
23. Oyster plate
24. Dessert plate
25. Winkle fork
26. Snail fork
27. Oyster fork
28. Lobster pick
29. Vegetable fork
30. Fish fork
31. Melon fork
32. Dinner fork
33. Turnip fork
34. Chestnut drill
35. Dinner plate
36. Salt cellar
37. Pepper attic
38. Meat knife
39. Fish knife
40. Fruit knife
41. Oyster knife
42. Pea knife
43. Bowie knife
44. Egg spoon
45. Soup spoon
46. Dessert spoon
47. Ice spoon
48. Tea spoon
49. Absinthe spoon
50. Cutlet bat
51. Pomegranate press
52. Meatball vice
53. Fly swatter
54. Crescent wrench
55. Stud finder
56. Potato gun

THE LANGUAGE OF FURNITURE

Antimacassar	dalliance
Armchair	remembrance
Armoire	unrequited love
Bookcase	amativeness
Carpet	loyalty
Chest of Drawers	purity
Coffee Table	affection
Drapes	jealousy
End Table	vanity
Fire Screen	honorable intentions
Floor Lamp	hot-bloodedness
Hall Tree	bile

Hassock	cupidity
Hatrack	idealism
Kitchen Chair	unwanted attention
Lawn Furniture	industry
Porch Swing	silent suffering
Sideboard	modesty
Sofa	desperation
Stepladder	hope
Table Lamp	regret
Throw Rug	love of country
Toaster	faith
Whatnot	coquetry

THE SEVEN DEADLY ARTS

bell ringing

experimental film

calligraphy

liturgical dance

mime

food styling

macramé

flyspray
half + half
corn flakes

Bob
767-8401

Tues 8:45

$$??

This is a test. For the next page, this book will conduct a test of the Emergency Publishing System. This is only a test.

This has been a test of the Emergency Publishing System. If this had been an actual emergency, this would have been an "instant book," designed to cash in on a major news event, celebrity scandal, or recent fad, while the market was hot. We now return you to your regularly scheduled book.

THIS PAGE IS BLANK

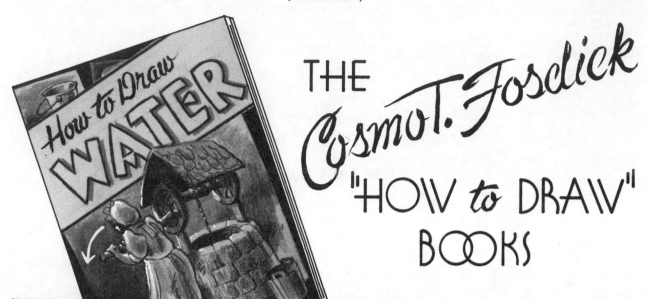

THE *Cosmo T. Fosdick* "HOW to DRAW" BOOKS

1. How to Draw Blood	19. How to Draw a Bath
2. How to Draw Fire	20. How to Draw Wire
3. How to Draw Attention	21. How to Draw a Salary
4. How to Draw Flies	22. How to Draw Criticism
5. How to Draw Lots	23. How to Draw Butter
6. How to Draw a Cart	24. How to Draw Current
7. How to Draw Water	25. How to Draw Abreast (adults only)
8. How to Draw Beer	26. How to Draw Cards
9. How to Draw Teeth	27. How to Draw Curtains
10. How to Draw Strings	28. How to Draw a Will
11. How to Draw a Blank	29. How to Draw Breath
12. How to Draw a Crowd	30. How to Draw Approval
13. How to Draw a Bead	31. How to Draw and Quarter
14. How to Draw a Bridge	32. How to Draw the Line
15. How to Draw Back a Bloody Stump	33. How to Draw Conclusions
16. How to Draw Straws	34. How to Draw to an End
17. How to Draw a Gun	35. How to Draw Out a Joke
18. How to Draw a Bow	

O HOLLYWOOD
O DISNEYLAND
O SAN SERIF
LACUNA BEACH
THE ART BOOK CAPITAL OF THE WORLD
O SANTA CLAUS

$3.95 EACH

Cosmo T. Fosdick Art Books

76 OILSPILL RD., LACUNA BEACH, CA 92657

Watch for these forthcoming titles in the . . . *Made Stupid* series:

Pruning Your Shrubs Made Stupid
Wok Cookery Made Stupid
Training Your Gerbil Made Stupid
Home Rewiring Made Stupid
Avoiding Probate Made Stupid
Sensual Foot Massage Made Stupid
Self-Hypnosis Made Stupid
Freemasonry Made Stupid
Acupuncture Made Stupid
Unicorns Made Stupid
The Bermuda Triangle Made Stupid
The Lost Books of the Bible Made Stupid
The Stupids Made Stupid
The Joy of Stupid
How Stupid Was My Valley
Lonely Are the Stupid
To Be Young, Gifted, and Stupid
When Stupid Things Happen to Good People
How Stupid Is Your Parachute?
The Making of Stupid: The Motion Picture
The Color Stupid

All titles will be uniform with the present volume, with the same hand-tooled, gold-stamped morocco leather bindings, marbled endpapers, and hand-tinted steel engravings on mould-made, 112 percent rag paper. Not sold in stores.